EMPOWERING RURAL WOMEN

EMPOWERING RURAL WOMEN

By

Sujit Kumar Dutta

Dilip Kumar Ghosh

AKANSHA PUBLISHING HOUSE

NEW DELHI-110 059 (INDIA)

AKANSHA PUBLISHING HOUSE
R-37B, Vani Vihar, Uttam Nagar,
New Delhi-110 0059 (INDIA)
Phone : 5640621
Email : ektabooks@yahoo.com

Empowering Rural Women
First Published 2002

ISBN 81-87606-28-2

PRINTED IN INDIA

Published by M.P. Misra for Akansha Publishing House, New Delhi and Printed at Mehra Offset Press, New Delhi.

Contents

Preface vii

1. Introduction 1

2. Profile of Women Workforce 8

3. Status of Female-Headed Household 32

4. Policies and Programmes Related to Women 53

5. Women Empowerment through Literacy 79

6. Women in Panchayat 96

Index 111

Preface

The complexity of the problem of women empowerment process itself requires both macro and micro considerations, and it is difficult to pass a judgment on its success by using a single or just a few selected criteria. The major discussion of empowerment process pertains mainly to the profile of women workforce, status of female-headed households, policies and programmes related to women, empowerment of women through literacy and women in panchayat. Hence, women empowerment has to be understood through these dimensions conjointly rather than in isolation.

The topics/themes included in this book analyse several interesting aspects of women empowerment issue. In the opening chapter the rationality of selected theme is reflected, while in the subsequent chapters it speaks on the issues in details, more specifically the chapters II and III speak about women-headed households and women workforce and their participation in the development process which was studied in comparison to the male counterpart in terms of non-workers and marginal workers. Further, the study also focuses on the agricultural and non-agricultural classes including their educational level. The status of female-headed household (FHH) is derived from the operational existence of FHH in comparison to total households of these ten villages under Birbhum District of West Bengal. Status was also determined through the socio-economic profile of their household including their assets, per annum income and their options to various self-employment programmes. It has been found that after having access to different poverty alleviation programmes they have not gone far ahead. Even the banks are reluctant to disburse credit with the apprehension that they may not get the money back. To combat this situation a sort of social action is necessary.

Chapter IV speaks about the different policies and programmes introduced by the government, which paved the way for the women not only to take decision regarding their role for their development in the rural areas, but in this process they become self-reliant. The shift of welfare-oriented programme for the women to development programme in the current era has placed the women in an advantageous position. The programme on 'Development of Women and Children in Rural Areas' has not only improved the status and quality of rural women but it has also enhanced their capacity in such a way that they can organise themselves and their work as well and in the long run, even if the programme is withdrawn, they will be able to sustain themselves. This is what is the expectation of the programme. This exploratory cum analytical study was carried out in all the seventeen districts of West Bengal.

In order to strengthen the programme further, it is suggested that the programme should be converged with other programmes, so that they reap larger benefits from the other programes too.

Chapter V is about the literacy, where the emphasis is given on the literacy programmes launched by which the women can be empowered. The awareness of women through literacy is the gateway of their involvement in the process of development by which they will be able to understand the programme, which is meant for but not imposed upon them. As a result they will never be dependent on the programme or even on implementers. This particular study was based on six blocks in the district of Birbhum.

Chapter VI (the last Chapter) is about the women in panchayat which means that the women are involved in maintaining panchayat not as dumb members but as vibrant leaders and motivators for the women at large. It is felt necessary to study the socio-economic background of the women leaders, which will enable us to select those leaders who could be the driving force to raise the status and position of women in the society. For the expository convenience the study was concentrated in three sub-divisions, out of which one block was chosen on the basis of highest population of that gram panchayat.

It emanates from the study that through the women reservation policy the women could enter into the local government not just as members only but they can address the matters related to their problems and take decision accordingly. Further, development however, depends on the backup support of the rural administrator in general and the block level bureaucracy in particular. It is also suggested to strengthen the knowledge of these women leaders at the block and the district level. This suggestion is given because the study reflects that understanding of panchayats and their role seems to be inadequate. Unless this situation is changed, the women will remain under the clutches of the male dominated society and the main purpose of empowering the women will be defeated.

The above chapters as mentioned were exclusive in nature. The conclusions drawn were also mentioned separately in each chapter. The drafts of this paper were presented in different national seminars and workshops. Each paper was written in sequence with the intention of making a volume of this kind.

Most of these papers were written at SIRD, West Bengal in consultation with Dr. Dilip Ghosh initially; later on it was improved here at the Regional Centre of NIRD, Guwahati. The authors would like to acknowledge the facilities offered by these institutions. The author is personally indebted to Mr. I. K. Bonia, who took the trouble to go through the entire draft manuscript, and Mr. Bhaskar Tahabildar for his continued assistance of checking the manuscript between the lines. Thanks are also due to Mr. A.J. Prabhat Meitei and Ms. Seema R. Das for their support in typing the manuscripts and Mr B.S. Dobal for the setting and designing it in the computer. Last but not the least I owe special gratitude to those officers and PR functionaries from the concerned districts who extended full cooperation in supplying the valuable information without which the study would not have been completed.

NIRD-NERC, **Sujit Kumar Dutta**
Guwahati

I

Introduction

Women empowerment especially in rural areas is a great concern to the thinkers, scholars and planners of the day. Numerous articles, books and write-ups are coming up these days, which are bringing interesting issues to the concerned community and are sensitizing their thinking about the empowerment of rural women. It is debatable whether the single factor determines the entire issue or not. If equitable access to resources is given to the rural women will it be possible to make rural women empowered? Else if decision-making powers are given to women will it make any sense to their empowerment? Further, if the status of women is raised will it bring more empowerment? Or simply we should protect the right of women in the society through legislation or act, reduce women atrocities giving more power to women through reservation in panchayat and or job reservation etc. Taking all these factors into consideration the present discussion will focus on major five issues mentioned below:

i. Profile of women workforce
ii. Status of Female Headed Households
iii. Policies and Programmes related to women
iv. Empowerment of women through literacy
v. Women in Panchayat

The brief details of the above issues are mentioned below:

i. Profile of Women Workforce

Women, especially in the rural areas have been surviving through ages by their services, whether it is recognized or not, still it is inherent in the very behaviour of rural women that they cannot stay free without any work. There is no denying the fact that there are records that an average Rajasthani woman work during peak farming season more than 16 hours a day. But the study on West Bengal has proved that the gainful employment to rural women is very much limited.

This is due to the fact that they are forced to stay back in their houses for giving their un-paid services. Looking at this pathetic condition of the women, the Eighth Five Year Plan emphasised especially women programmes to make women equal partners and participants in the development programmes. At the grass root levels the programmes are for women's organistion and groups. Further, through the 72nd and 73rd Constitutional Amendments, the empowerment of women issues were tackled through access of women to education, training, credit and productive and sustained employment opportunities. But things at large remain at the stage of passing resolutions and setting up of Committees and Commissions only, which may not bring about any change or improvement in the status of women workforce in the countryside.

ii. Status of Female Headed Households

The Female Headed Households are generally living in a closed circuit of economic deprivations, illiteracy and lack of exposure in understanding their position in the society. Their status remains the same, even after launching massive poverty alleviation programmes in the countryside. The study shows that out of 178 female-headed households in the West Bengal villages, none of them received assistance under IRDP within twelve years of its operation. Even the Bankers feel that these families may not run the scheme efficiently and consequently may not be able to repay the Bank dues.

iii. Policies and Programmes Related to Women

A serious thought was given to Women Development right from the inception of the plan era in 1951, and till 1971 it was only on welfare aspect. It was during the sixth Five Year Plan that a chapter was included on 'Women and Development', and a series of programes on women were recommended, one of which was Development of Women and Children in Rural Areas (DWCRA), started in the year 1982-83 with a focus on:

— improving the status and quality of poor rural women and their children;
— improving their earning capacity through income generating activities;
— improving the impact of on - going development programmes in rural areas through their integration and convergence;
— Organising women for planning and implementing the development programmes for them;
— Self-subsistence even after withdrawal of assistance.

All these taken together are expected to lead to their empowerment and enhancement of status.

It has been found that the programme is yet to achieve its success as expected, the reason being that the programme is yet to be understood as a group programme and /or activity rather than individual one. Further, many of the functionaries or programme implementers like APOs (DWCRA), BDOs and Gram Sevikas do not have a clear understanding of the objectives of the programme. Hence, to empower the women groups it is imperative to empower these functionaries or agents first, and then to inculcate this into the minds of the programme beneficiaries. Moreover, in the overall set-up of development administration, DWCRA programme is receiving low priority. Hence, the programme must be viewed not as a token of sympathy for the rural poor women but as programmes in the greater interest of the society as the problem of women in society is the problem of the society as a whole. The official functionaries most often fail to internalize reasons for the deprivation of women, and therefore accept the programme like other routine work. It has to be understood that women have enough potentialities to carry out any type of work independently; the only thing required from the rural development agencies is a kind of continuous support and services so that they may turn into strong vibrant groups. In order to strengthen the DWCRA groups, convergence with other programmes is essential, so that they are able to derive benefit from other programmes as well. Hence, programme beneficiaries should be made aware of the benefit of the programme properly, so that they are able to take proper interest; then their participation will automatically be assured. Even this work may be entrusted to Voluntary Organisations as they have rich experiences in these fields. For better performance of the programme constant care and support from all associated with rural development are absolutely necessary.

iv. Empowerment of Women Through Literacy

The major findings of this study are that to acquire any benefit from any scheme, the rural poor need to be literate through the total Literacy Programme. Eventually they will be able to understand that there are programmes, which are meant for them.

Because of illiteracy many programmes meant for the beneficiaries may not be considered in true sense as their own programmes but at times are regarded as imposed. As a result of this the beneficiaries become more dependent on the programme implementers and subsequently a kind of domination and subordination relationship develops between the beneficiaries and the programme implementers. Under these circumstances the beneficiaries remain in isolation and content with whatever they are given. Hence, a drive for making rural poor literate through total literacy campaign is indispensable in order to reap the benefits of the various schemes of rural development.

v. Women in Panchayat

The women in panchayat do not merely speak about the reservation of women seats in the panchayat as per 73rd Amendment Act 1992. The major focus of this theme is on the socio-economic background of the women Panchayat leaders. This is precisely done in order to determine their status and position in the society. The study was concentrated in only one district and all the three tiers of the panchayat. As revealed by the study, quite a lot of new members entered into the panchayat due to the reservation policy, but back-up support from both rural development administration and block level bureaucracy is inadequate. A constant interaction with the senior members of the panchayat and continuous training at the block and district level are required to strengthen their knowledge.

While interviewing a few emerging young leaders of panchayat it has been found that their understanding of Panchayat Raj System is poor and they are yet to understand their role clearly. They are still dependent on the officials either at block or district level for almost every activity. But the very purpose of brining women into panchayat is to free them from the clutches of the dependency of male dominating society, or in other words from subordinate condition to equality. Otherwise the very purpose of empowering them will be defeated. The women empowerment in the countryside will largely depend on the empowerment of their representative new leaders, who should be equipped with adequate knowledge about the Panchayat Raj and their definite role to empower the women at large to prove themselves as equal partners in the society.

Apart from taking up these issues it is also necessary to understand why we focus on the women. The reasons are as follows:

Women constitute one half of the population in the society. We cannot afford to keep them out of the mainstream. As per

1991 census 407.1 million females are there in our country as against total population of 846.3 million; 297.8 million live in the rural areas and 27 per cent of them live below poverty line (roughly 11 million).

Secondly, they are productive workers in India's national economy, as they constitute 1/3 of the labour force.

Thirdly, the poorer the family, the greater is the dependence on women's economic productivity. Hence, enhancing their economic productivity is an important strategy for improving the welfare of 60 million Indian households living below the poverty line.

Fourthly, it has been found that there is significant gap between women's, especially rural women's potential and actual productivity. The productivity gap of the poor women is much wider than that of the poor men. Therefore, women would gain proportionately more, if investment allocation and development efforts shifted in their favour.

Fifthly, women's earning has a positive correlation with children's health, nutrition and education level. Studies have shown that Indian women contribute a much larger share of their earnings to basic family maintence than men. Improving women's productivity, income and quality of life, implies a multi dimensional contribution for their overall growth and development. Apart from socio-economic and political empowerment to make rural women effective, initiative should be taken to clear the psychological cobwebs, which they have been suffering due to life long social taboos and gender prejudices. While adopting strategies for empowering women, (rural women in particular) these constraints have to be taken into consideration.

Women's involvement in the planning and management of any programme is indispensable, and at the same time they have to be involved with the community organisations. Along with the awareness programme there should be some local organizations/institutions, which should organize the rural poor women and help strengthen the rural women groups in order to make them self-sustenant. In Society prioritizing women's needs and sensitization of an advocacy for gender is immensely important. It is also necessary to change the attitude and mentality of both men and women towards their relationship, which should be more of complimentary in nature than contradictory. Emphasis on harmonization of thoughts and actions and acceptance of women as positive companion and not a liability would create a sense of belonging and instill confidence in them.

Whatever domestic work the women folk do is not being accounted in the computation of national income. If their services in the form of domestic work could be monetised, (converted into money) their contribution to our national income would be greater.

However, the details are mentioned in the subsequent chapters, which are data based, and support the statement and argument put forward in this introductory chapter.

II

Profile of Women Workforce

A society ravaged with inequity between males and females cannot ensure prosperity for adequate decent living. In spite of this eternal truth in a male dominated society, productive power of women remains unrecognized. Women are mostly engaged in household activities which are not considered 'economic' and therefore, do not get counted as workers under conventional measures of employment (Batra, 1996). In this regard the eminent agricultural Scientist Swaminathan mentioned that more than 50 per cent of farm work particularly those involving drudgery and long hours is performed by women in India. Much of their work is both unrecognised and unpaid (Swaminathan, 1995). As per UNDP's report, the value of women's 'hidden contribution' to the global economy exceeds 11 trillions (Human Development Report, 1995). Only the reproductive capacity of women got due recognition. In the words of Swami Vivekananda, they (women) were turned into 'manufacturing machines' to produce children. Intra family division of labour adds further fuel to the fire.

The intention of the present study is to focus on the scenario of women participation in the total labour force in rural areas. The labour force participation rate for rural women is twice that of urban women (41.2 per cent and 20.2 per cent respectively). On the other hand in the case of men, it is much higher in both rural and urban areas and not much different from each other (89 per cent and 83.3 per cent in rural and urban areas respectively). Further, the labour force participation rate for women in the age group 5+ are similarly quite low both in rural (29.3 per cent) and urban areas (14.7 per cent), the overall rate being 26 per cent; and these are substantially lower than the corresponding rates for men (Batra, *op.cit,*:pp.16-17). The recently completed 2001 census brought to the limelight a grim fact that the rate of female workforce in total working population in India in urban and rural areas is 9.73 percent and 27.06 percent respectively. 75 percent of the female workers in industries are paid between Rs.5 to Rs.7 a day and in many cases nothing is paid to them. Whatever is paid taken away by tout who brings those girls paying some loan and advance to their parents (see Assam Tribune, 2002).

The present study is based on the Birbhum District of West Bengal state, and the district is having predominant rural characteristic. For expository convenience the study is restricted to one district only. Data sources are mainly from the District Census handbooks, However, for the purpose of analysis the Panchayat functionaries of the concerned district along with a few women workforce were also consulted in order to get an overview of the status and condition of women workforce.

Objectives of the Study

The major thrust of this article is to study the work participation of rural female and this was also understood in terms of male participation and other non-working women, main workers and marginal workers. Secondly classification of workers is made on the basis of both agricultural and non-agricultural classes of the workforce. Classification is also made on the basis of educational level. Finally, the age structure of female workers, which determines the level of participation of women workforce in comparison to male partner, has also been considered. Secondly, Matriculation/ Secondary/Higher Secondary/Intermediate/Pre-University, Non-Technical Diploma or Certificate not equals to degree, Technical diploma or certificate not equal to degree and Graduation or above form the basis for classification.

Work Participation Rates of Rural Women

The concept of work and broad categorization of population on that basis underwent different changes from census to census since 1951. For example, in 1951 census the basis of classification was income. This was a continuation of 1931 census where population was divided into three classes viz., earner, working dependent and non- working dependent.

Even persons who were not working actually but receiving income from land, property etc. were classified as economically active. Following this principle basically, 1951 census introduced a change where classification of population was made in three categories of self supporting person, earning dependent and non-earning dependent. According to 1951 census, a self supporting person was one who was in receipt of an income and that income was sufficient at least for his own maintenance; earning dependent was a person who earned income, but that was not sufficient for his own maintenance. Self supporting and earning dependent groups are clubbed together as earning members. Thus, in before 1961 census, the element of income or the criterion of economic independence was adopted for measuring the economic activity of an individual. But in 1961 census, economic data were collected on the basis of work pursued by an individual. "The person engaged in productive work irrespective of their deriving any income or not have been graded as workers in 1961 census (District Census Hand book, Birbhum, 1961-66). According to this concept, persons including family workers and children working but not earning enough to maintain themselves had also been considered as workers. Therefore, in 1961 census, "Any person who generally spends more than one hour per day on any particular productive occupation has been included amongst working population. In respect of seasonal work like cultivation, livestock, household industry etc. person, having regular work for more than an hour a day throughout the greater part of the working season have been treated as workers" (*ibid.*). Persons who were not engaged in any economic activity were treated as non-worker. According to 1971 census, a worker was defined as a person whose main activity was participation in any economically productive work by his physical or mental activity where work involved not only the actual work but also effective supervision and direction of work. In 1981 census the whole population was divided into three categories viz. main workers, marginal workers and non-workers.

The main worker was defined as a person whose main activity was participation in any economically productive work by his physical or mental activities and who had worked for 183 days or more in a year. A non-worker was defined as a person who had not done any work at any time. A marginal worker (this concept was introduced for the first time) is a person who worked for less than 183 days. Thus the concept of work was concretized with greater real base only in 1981 census. 1991 census followed the path of 1981. In 1991 census instructions to enumerators it has been clearly laid down to take sufficient care in recording responses of women as "women are often classified as non workers because of non reporting of their work. It also happens that women who work for the major part of the year are reported as working for less than six months" (Census of India, 1991:33).

In the backdrop of these conceptual exercises let us now go into analysis of statistical data of five censuses (1951-1991) since independence of the country. Provisional figures of 1991 census are collected from the District Census Office to give the current status of women participation in work force. In 1951 out of 494801 rural females only 46851 were self-supporting females i.e., 9.46 per cent . And 85.58 per cent were non-earning dependents. If earning but dependent females be considered then total earning females were 71344 i.e. 14.41 per cent of total rural females. In spite of very liberal definition of a worker in 1961 census in the rural sector, the district labour participation by both males and females had been very low. Only 51.70 per cent of males and 9.6 per cent of females were classed as workers. Police Station-wise work participation rates (WPR) of rural females are given in Table 1 below:

Table 1
Work Participation Rates of Rural Females 1961-1991

Sl.No.	*Police Station*	*1961*	*1971*	*1981*	*1991*
1.	Murarai	6.50	3.01	4.36	3.48
2.	Nalhati	6.39	2.79	6.87	3.92
3.	Rampurhat	12.78	4.90	9.87	8.20
4.	Mayureswar	8.56	4.31	8.57	7.88
5.	Mahammad Bazar	17.26	6.76	17.27	16.33
6.	Rajnagar	13.65	6.61	16.09	14.91
7.	Khoyrasole	14.63	4.12	10.04	7.42
8.	Dubrajpur	12.92	5.39	10.54	12.07
9.	Suri	8.60	4.58	11.29	10.07
10.	Illambazar	10.89	5.94	7.99	8.92
11.	Sainthia	8.82	4.90	10.98	12.23
12.	Bolpur	12.09	8.35	16.29	16.45
13.	Labhpur	4.73	1.54	3.32	4.01
14.	Nanoor	4.37	2.29	3.58	4.25
	Total	9.64	4.38	9.02	8.35

Source: District Census Handbook of Birbhum District 1961, 1971 & 1981.

WPR is calculated by the following formula:

$$\text{WPR} = \frac{\text{Female Workers}}{\text{Total Female}} \times 100$$

In case of 1981 and 1991 censuses main workers and marginal workers are added to get total workers. Form Table 1 below, it can be seen that in Mahammed Bazar Police Station 17.26 per cent females were engaged as workers in 1961 against the district figure of 9.64 per cent in seven police station areas.

WPR of rural females were below the district average. In Labhpur and Nanoor, WPR is the lowest. In the district head quarter Suri, the ratio of female workers is below the district average. In Muslim dominated areas of the district e.g. Murarai and Nalhati police station, participation of female in work continues to be very low since 1961. Even in 1991 it is 3.48 and 3.92 per cent respectively, which is less than the district average of 8.35 per cent. In Bolpur police station area participation of women in workforce is more or less maintaining an increasing trend with exception in 1971 census only. In Bolpur area over the period 1961-1991, a growth of 1.20 per cent in WPR per annum is noticed. This becomes possible due to emergence of different cottage industries and handicrafts in and around Santiniketan. Due to definitional inflexibilities in 1971 census WPR of females in the district declined to 4.38 per cent. 1971 figures in Table 1 are calculated on the basis of main activity only.

In 1981 census, however, it improved, but again in 1991 census it is reduced. In comparison to 1981 census, in 1991 WPR of females decreased in eight police station areas. These are Murarai, Nalhati, Rampurhat, Mayureshwar, Mahammad Bazar, Rajnagar, Khuyrasole and Suri. Taking the district as a whole decade variations of WPR for rural females are (-) 54.56 per cent during 1961-71, (+) 105.93 per cent during 1971-1981 and again (-) 7.42 per cent during 1981-91.

Proportion of non-working female population during 1961-1991 is presented in Table 2 below. From the table it can be seen that during 1961-1991 period percentage of non-working females has been reduced from 90.35 in 1961 to 86.52 in 1991 i.e. 4.23 over a period of thirty years. Per annum decrease, thus, becomes 0.14 per cent. Certainly this is very negligible. Introduction of several special employment programmes particularly during sixth and seventh five-year plan do not bring in appreciable reduction in numbers of non-working females. Within ten years of 1981-1991, proportion of non-working rural females has been reduced by 4.46 per cent i.e. per annum reduction of 0.45 per cent. It was reduced by 4.64 per cent between 1971-1981. These two figures indicate that during the two decades of 1971-1981 and 1981-1991, proportion of non-working rural females got reduced more or less at a constant rate. In 1981 census, in eight police station areas was proportions of non-working rural females were below the district average of 90.98 per cent. But from figures of 1991 census, though it is reflected that in all police stations non-working female population is getting reduced, yet only five police stations have less proportion of non working rural female than district average. This signifies that proportion of non-working females does not decrease appreciably in all areas of the district.

Table 2
Proportion of Non-working Rural Female Population vis-a-vis Total Rural Female 1961-1991 (in percentage)

Sl.No.	*Police Station*	*1961*	*1971*	*1981*	*1991*
1.	Murarai	93.50	96.98	95.64	93.04
2.	Nalhati	93.45	97.21	92.85	94.87
3.	Rampurhat	87.21	95.10	90.12	70.35
4.	Mayureswar	94.43	95.69	91.42	88.59
5.	Mahammad Bazar	82.73	93.24	82.73	77.99
6.	Rajnagar	86.34	93.38	83.91	78.58
7.	Khoyrasole	85.37	95.88	89.95	85.08
8.	Dubrajpur	87.07	94.60	89.45	77.49
9.	Suri	91.39	95.41	88.70	82.50
10.	Illambazar	89.10	94.05	92.01	86.02
11.	Sainthia	91.18	95.09	89.01	81.93
12.	Bolpur	87.91	91.65	83.70	78.90
13.	Labhpur	95.27	97.71	96.41	93.46
14.	Nanoor	95.63	98.45	96.67	93.29
	Total	90.35	95.62	90.98	86.52

Source: District Census Handbook of 1961,1971 & 1981 Census

In Table 3 rural female-work force and non-working rural female in proportion to rural population of the district are presented. Figures for five census statistics are given. From the Table it can be said that female work force per 100 of total population was reduced from 7.15 in 1951 to 4.07 in 1991. In 1971 due to difference in definitions and concept of work and reference periods, index of female work-force suffered a lot. It improved in 1981 and slid down again in 1991. Non-working females per hundred of total rural females were reduced very marginally in between four decades since 1951. Though during forty years since 1951, population in rural areas of the district increases 2.33 times, females work-force increased by 1.33 times during the same period. Non-working females increase by 2.31 times during the period.

Table 3
Rural Female Work Force & Non-working Female to total Rural Population of the District: 1951-1991

Sl. No.	*Year*	*Rural Population*	*Total Female workers*	*Percentage*	*Total Female Non-workers*	*Percentage*
1.	1951	997896	71344	7.15	423457	42.43
2.	1961	1345389	64327	4.78	602787	44.80
3.	1971	1651137	35895	2.17	778899	47.17
4.	1981	1922296	85199	4.43	859286	44.70
5.	1991	2326237	94701	4.47	980734	42.16

In Table 4, sex ratio (female population per 1000 male workers) and female non-workers per 1000 of male non-workers are presented. Figures for all the five censuses are given to have a comparative view. Table 4 reflects that female ratio in the district decreases from one census period to another (only exception in 1961). Female ratio in employment dwindles till 1971 from 1951 census and again rose from 1981. On the other hand, female ratio in non-working population increased in 1961 over 1951 and then fell in 1971. Again it increased in 1981 over 1971 and then fell in 1991. During 1981-1991, reduction of female non-workers per 1000 of male non-workers is 4.37 cent only.

Table 4
Rural Female Workers & Non-workers per thousand of Males (1951-1991)

Sl.No.	*Year*	*Sex Ratio*	*Female workers*	*Female Non-workers*
1.	1951	983	258	1868
2.	1961	984	180	1879
3.	1971	973	88	1805
4.	1981	965	107	1830
5.	1991	950	152	1750

Sex-Ratio: Female Population per 1000 of males.

Classification of Women Workers

In 1951 census the population of the district were mainly divided into two broad livelihood categories viz. the agricultural classes and non-agricultural classes. Agricultural classes were further sub-divided into four classes as below:

(i) Cultivators of land wholly or mainly owned and their dependents:
(ii) Cultivators of land wholly or mainly not owned and their dependents;
(iii) Cultivating labourers and their dependents; and
(iv) Non-cultivating owners of land, agricultural rent receivers and their dependents.

Non-agricultural classes were divided into following four classes on the basis of the principal means of livelihood:

(i) Production other than cultivation;

(ii) Commerce;
(iii) Transport; and
(iv) Other services and miscellaneous services.

1961 Census classified working population on the basis of their economic activity. Concept of dependency was abandoned with the adoption of the concept of work. Nine categories of workers had been made in this census

(i) Cultivator,
(ii) Agricultural labourer,
(iii) Mining, quarrying, livestock, forestry, fishing, hunting and plantations, Orchards and allied activities
(iv) Household industry,
(v) Manufacturing other than household industry,
(vi) Construction,
(vii) Trade and Commerce,
(viii) Transport, storage and communications and
(ix) Other services.

In 1971 census, more or less 1961 classification was followed. The only change caused was in No. (3) Category wherefrom mining and quarrying was taken out to make a separate category. No. 4 and 5 were clubbed together under a broad category of manufacturing, processing, servicing and repairs. Overall in 1971 there were nine categories of workers. 1981 and 1991 censuses followed the same path.

In table 5, percentage break up of rural female workforce is presented. From the table it can be seen that proportion of women cultivators is gradually descending.

Over the period of 1951-1991, percentage variation in women cultivators is minus 66.18. On the other hand proportion of women agricultural labourers increase by 138.23 percent. This indicates two things: one, control of women over land

Table 5
Break-up of Rural Female Work Force (in percentage)

Sl.No.	*Category*	*1951*	*1961*	*1971*	*1981*	*1991*
1.	Cultivators	43.17	26.18	13.58	15.25	14.60
2.	Agricultural Labours	26.60	42.38	63.96	64.87	63.37
3.	Livestock, forestry, etc.	—	1.89	0.77	0.73	—
4.	Mining & Quarrying	—	—	0.30	0.68	—
5.	Household Industry	16.17	14.45	3.65	7.80	8.35
6.	Other than household Industry	—	4.33	4.10	2.81	—
7.	Construction	—	0.70	0.22	0.10	—
8.	Trade & Commerce	1.72	1.45	1.87	1.02	13.68
9.	Transport, etc.	0.70	—	0.75	0.09	—
10.	Other services	12.24	9.25	10.80	6.65	—

Source: Birbhum District Census Handbook of 1951, 1961, 1971 and 1981 Census.

decreases and second, women are coming out in large number to sell out their labour in agricultural operations. In household industry also share of women workers decreased in between the period 1961-1981; from 14.45 percent in 1961 it fell to 7.80 percent in 1981; variation in percentage terms is minus 46.02 percent. According to census terminology, household industry is 'an industry conducted by the head of the household himself/herself and or by the members of the household at home or within the village. In rural areas the industry should not be run on the scale of a registered factory, which would qualify or has to be registered under the Indian Factories Act (Census, 1981:23). Combining household and other than household industry, proportion of women workers reduced from 16.17 in 1951 to 8.35 in 1991 i.e. over forty years period change in proportion was to the tune of minus 48.36 percent. This signifies male subordination and lack of opportunities for women to take up enterprising activities. Introduction of various self-employment programmes does not change the scenario. In between 1981 and 1991 proportion of women workers in household and other than household industries sector was reduced from 10.61 percent in 1981 to 8.35 percent in 1991. This accounts for reduction of 21.30 percent. The majority of female workers in household industry sector are engaged in processing of crops (such as from paddy to rice, muri making etc.), bidi rolling, cane-bamboo handicrafts silk and cotton textile, spinning and reeling, different artistic handiworks etc. Share of trade and commerce, transport, storage etc. and other services in total women work force is also not so substantial. Involvement of women in different tertiary sector however is gradually picking up since 1961 (exception being 1981 census). In comparison to 1951 census, however it fell marginally in 1991 census; variation is minus 2.70 per cent.

Table 6

Sex- Ratio of workers

Sl.No.	*Category*	*1951*	*1961*	*1971*	*1981*	*1991*
1.	Cultivators	217	94	30	37	54
2.	Agricultural Labours	211	250	140	181	265
3.	Livestock, Forestry, etc.	—	115	80	64	—
4.	Mining & Quarrying	—	—	82	142	—
5.	Household Industry	840	857	139	268	364
6.	Other than household Industry	—	467	183	115	—
7.	Construction	—	25	54	29	—
8.	Trade & Commerce	203	108	61	32	107
9.	Transport, Storage etc.	68	—	52	9	—
10.	Other services	344	199	92	118	—

It appears from the analysis so far made that working women in this district are not in keeping with their total number. Though in this district in 1991, for every 1000 males there are 950 females, but amongst the working population for every 1000 males there are only 151 females. In Table 6 category-wise sex ratio of workers (female workers per thousand of males) is given so as to indicate women participation in different works vis-à-vis male participation.

From the table it can be seen that number of women as cultivators decreases from 217 in 1951 to 54 in1991. Between 1971 and 1991, however, it increased by a margin of 80 percent. Sex ratio of agricultural labourers in 1991 is so far the highest since independence. According to 1991 census, there are 265 women per thousand of male agricultural labourers. Women in Birbhum generally find favourable employment as agricultural labourers as the district is predominately agricultural. Representation of women in activities like trade and commerce, transport, storage etc. and other services is minimal. For example, in 1981 there were only 9 women per thousand of males in transport, storage, and communication class of workers. In industrial class (household and other than household taken together) sex ratio of workers declined from 840 in 1951 to 364 in 1991 i.e. decline of 56.67 percent.

Table 7
Sectoral break-up of female workforce 1951-1991
(in percentage)

Year	*Sectors*		
	Primary	*Secondary*	*Tertiary*
1951	69.77	16.17	14.06
1961	69.56	19.67	10.77
1971	78.31	8.05	13.64
1981	80.85	11.29	7.86
1991	77.97	8.35	13.68

In Table 7 break-up of female workforce on the basis of broad sectoral activities (Primary, Secondary and Tertiary) is given. Involvement of women in primary sector increased from 69.77 per cent in 1951 to 77.97 percent in 1991 i.e., a rise of 11.71 percent. In 1981 it reached the peak of 80.85 percent. On the other hand, secondary sector proportion of women employment was reduced from 16.17 percent in 1951 to 8.35 percent in 1991; reduction is to the extent of 48.36 percent. Participation of women in tertiary sector activities (service and business) was reduced by a margin of 2.70 percent in 1991 census in comparison to 1951. In 1981, share in this sector touched the lowest figure (7.86 percent). In between 1981-1991 share of women workers in this sector rose by 74.04 percent. This becomes possible due to increasing coverage of women under service-business sector of different self-employment programmes. In addition to it, women are gradually interested to undertake diversified activities involving certain amount of risks and enterprises. In Table 8 sectoral sex ratio (sectoral female workers per thousand of males) for the period 1951-1991 is given.

Table 8
Sectoral break-up of female workers per 1000 males
1951-1991

Year	*Sectors*		
	Primary	*Secondary*	*Tertiary*
1951	214.00	840 00	205.00
1961	138.00	719.00	164.00
1971	83.00	134.00	65.00
1981	94.00	175.00	63.00
1991	159.00	364.00	107.00

In tertiary sector, sex ratio is always low in comparison with other two sectors. Sex ratio in secondary sector is always the highest in all censuses. Involvement of women in secondary sector is always the highest which is, on the one hand, due to large number of rice mills employing more women labour than men, and on the other, existence of large number of handicraft and cottage industries demanding more women workers than men.

Workers Classification by Education Level

In Table 9, female workers are classified on the basis of attainment of educational status. The rural female workers of the district seem to be slow in attainment of literacy.

Table 9

Classification of Female workers on the basis of educational Status 1961-1991 (in percentage)

Sl.No.	*Educational Level*	*1961*	*1971*	*1981*	*1991*
1.	Illiterate	97.47	89.55	92.69	86.74
2.	Literate	2.53	10.45	7.31	13.26
	Literates without Education levels	1.79	4.73	1.46	2.73
a)	Primary	0.52	3.28	2.23	4.22
b)	Middle	X	0.81	0.97	2.18
c)	Matriculation or Higher Secondary	0.22	1.45	X	1.38
d)	Matriculation or Secondary	X	X	1.21	X
e)	Matriculation or Higher Secondary/ Pre-University	X	X	0.41	0.72
f)	Non-Technical Diploma or Certificate not equal to degree	X	0.02	X	X
g)	Technical Diploma or Certificate not equal to degree	X	X	0.14	0.07
h)	Graduate or above	X	0.16	0.89	1.96

Source: District Census Handbook of 1961,1971, West Bengal Series part III A & B (i), 1991.

In 1961 census about 97.47 percent of female workers in rural areas were illiterate. Over the period of twenty years, this level of illiteracy was reduced by a margin of only 4.90 percent. In 1991 census overall female illiteracy stood at 71.24 percent. Again of the literate women, 70.75 percent had no formal education. However, in 1971 census literate women workers without any education stood at 45.26 percent of literates.

In 1981 this figure further slid down to 19.97 percent of literates. This indicates involvement of more women in formal education. Of the literate female workers in 1961, 20.55 percent attained primary level of education while in 1971 and 1981 corresponding figures were 31.38 percent and 30.50 percent. According to 1961 census illiterate is a person 'who can neither read nor write or can merely read but cannot write in any language' and 'literate is a person who can both read and write with understanding'. The same definitions are maintained in later censuses also. In 1961 census, educational levels are classified into four groups viz. (a) illiterate, (b) literate (without education levels), (c) Primary or junior basic and (d) matriculation and above. But in 1971 and 1981 more classifications were introduced to get a vivid picture. In Table 10, sectoral classification of rural female labour force on the basis of literacy level is presented. Census data of 1961, 1971, 1981 and 1999 were taken.

For 1951 no such classification was available. From the Table it can be visualized that within workers of primary sector heavy illiteracy prevails since 1961 days. Between 1961 and 1981 illiteracy of primary sector workers was reduced by a margin of only 0.50 percent. Within the same period a margin of 13.42 percent and that of tertiary sector reduced illiteracy of secondary sector workers by 41.62 percent. Women having qualifications of graduation and above are mostly engaged in tertiary sector activities. From 1.74 percent this increased to 11.10 percent i.e. an increase of 6.38 times. Female workers having formal education are mostly engaged in secondary and tertiary sector works. This fact reflects that with enhancement in educational status, women are taking up such activities, which

Table 10

Sectoral Classification of Rural Female Workers by literacy Status: 1961-1991

Educational Level	*1961*			*1971*			*1981*			*1991*		
	P	*S*	*T*	*P*	*S*	*T*	*P*	*S*	*T*	*P*	*S*	*T*
Illiterate	98.30	96.05	94.48	92.94	78.14	69.79	97.72	83.16	54.50	77.92	63.01	52.58
Literate without educational level	1.42	2.99	2.15	4.35	4.66	8.13	0.80	5.65	2.13	11.04	25.50	28.08
Primary and middle	2.26	0.94	1.38	2.54	10.03	12.20	1.32	10.42	11.94	10.71	11.06	10.59
Matriculation or above	0.02	0.02	1.99	0.17	7.16	7.85	0.14	0.77	18.42	0.29	0.38	5.27
Graduate and above	X	X	X	X	X	1.74	0.02	X	11.10	0.04	0.05	3.30
Non technical diploma not equal to degree	X	X	X	X	X	0.29	X	X	X	X	X	0.02
Technical diploma not equal to degree	X	X	X	X	X	X	X	X	1.91	X	X	0.16

P-Primary Sector S-Secondary Sector T-Tertiary Sector

involve skills, risk and entrepreneurship. This is corroborated by the statistics that only 0.02 percent workers of primary sector in 1981 are graduates.

Age Structure of Female Workers

In Table 11 age group-wise classification of female workers of different industrial category and non-workers are made. The Table is constructed on the basis of census statistics of 1961, 1971,1981 and 1991.

Table 11
Age group-wise classification of Female Workers per 100 Workers

Category	*Age Bracket*	*1961*	*1971*	*1981*	*1991*
Total Workers	A	15.25	9.70	12.05	7.85
	B	15.10	8.50	10.54	12.79
	C	15.91	7.35	8.19	14.95
	D	15.56	8.10	9.80	12.94
Cultivators	A	15.95	2.87	4.92	2.83
	B	8.72	1.95	3.74	2.70
	C	8.51	3.63	3.42	2.89
	D	8.53	2.63	3.62	2.74
Agricultural Labour	A	20.92	11.55	13.53	7.25
	B	21.92	13.41	16.10	6.86
	C	18.03	10.76	14.73	5.93
	D	20.33	12.59	15.75	6.46
Plantations & Allied Agriculture	A	3.83	3.19	3.88	1.25
	B	10.65	7.17	5.83	1.39
	C	21.83	11.47	7.70	2.74
	D	13.75	8.42	6.40	4.32

Contd...

contd...

Category	*Age Bracket*	*1961*	*1971*	*1981*	*1991*
Household Industry	A	28.31	19.24	46.65	31.53
	B	44.28	12.20	22.62	17.42
	C	51.22	11.78	17.02	10.68
	D	47.44	12.05	20.77	14.83
Manufacturing Industry	A	40.32	28.57	20.68	12.76
	B	25.84	15.10	10.56	8.12
	C	39.75	14.08	8.79	3.46
	D	31.10	14.79	10.02	4.35
Construction	A	21.42	4.76	X	0.85
	B	1.74	6.11	3.54	3.35
	C	3.01	3.44	2.35	2.09
	D	2.28	5.08	3.03	2.12
Trade and Commerce	A	22.88	11.91	6.46	7.23
	B	7.05	4.45	2.60	2.85
	C	11.51	6.77	3.95	4.13
	D	9.12	5.27	3.04	2.59
Transport, Storage & Communication	A	X	23.07	X	7.56
	B	X	5.02	1.26	1.16
	C	X	4.08	0.29	0.54
	D	X	4.74	0.96	0.83
Other Service	A	9.54	8.44	19.29	16.32
	B	15.09	7.45	12.76	17.86
	C	19.45	8.31	6.68	9.25
	D	16.95	7.73	10.40	11.43
Non-workers	A	50.23	50.06	50.60	86.68
	B	86.60	82.74	80.12	77.96

contd...

contd...

Category	*Age Bracket*	*1961*	*1971*	*1981*	*1991*
	C	94.27	94.13	94.31	76.08
	D	89.38	85.82	83.70	78.09

Note: A, B, C and D are explained in the text under the section Age Structure of female workers.

Source: 1) District Census Handbook of 1961,1971
2) Census Publication- West Bengal Series part III A & B (i), 1991.

Age brackets taken up for construction of the table (11) are the following:

A : 0-34 years of all censuses

B : 15-34 years of 1961 census
15-39 years 1971, 1981,and 1991 census

C : 35-59 years of 1961 census
40-49 years of 1971 and 1981, and 1991 census

D : 15-59 years of 1961, 1971,1981 and 1991 census

From the Table it can be seen that in comparison to 1961 period proportion of women workers dropped in all age groups. In contrast to this general trend, in household industry, in 0-14 years age groups, proportion of female workers shot up to 46.65 percent. However in this same category with increase in age bracket, the proportion declines abruptly. In 15-59 years age group this decline in 1981 is to the extent of 56.22 per cent. This reflects continuing apathy and neglect of potentiality of women power, as they grow older. As women grew older, in rural areas they were mostly removed from work mainly for the social obligations thrusted upon them. Thus, it can safely be emphasized that women power is still either largely unutilised or imprudently utilised even after more than three decades of independence. The only happy sign is that progressively women are taking up diversified activities of tertiary sector. Proportion of female non-workers is also gradu-

Table 12

Rural Female Workers per 100 Male Workers in Main Industrial Categories Classified by broad Age Groups: 1961-1981

Category	*1961*				*1971*				*1981*			
	A	*B*	*C*	*D*	*A*	*B*	*C*	*D*	*A*	*B*	*C*	*D*
Total Workers	17.78	18.92	17.82	18.43	10.74	9.29	7.93	8.82	13.70	11.79	8.91	10.87
Non-workers	100.93	645.70	16.45	8.42	100.25	479.46	1.603.47	605.50	1.024.44	103.19	1660.12	513.66
Cultivators	18.98	9.55	9.30	9.43	2.95	1.99	3.77	2.70	5.17	3.88	3.54	3.76
Agricultural Labour	26.45	28.08	22.00	25.53	13.06	15.48	12.06	14.41	15.52	19.20	17.27	18.69
Plantations & Allied Agriculture	3.89	12.09	28.60	16.21	3.30	7.73	12.96	9.19	4.04	5.83	8.35	6.55
Household Industry	39.49	79.49	105.02	90.26	23.83	13.90	13.70	13.70	87.45	29.24	20.51	26.22
Manufacturing	67.56	34.85	65.98	45.14	40.00	17.79	16.40	17.36	26.06	11.81	9.63	11.14
Construction	27.27	1.77	3.10	2.33	5.00	6.51	3.50	5.36	X	3.67	2.40	3.12
Trade and Commerce	29.67	7.59	13.01	10.03	13.52	4.65	7.26	5.27	6.90	2.67	4.12	3.14
Transport, Storage & Communication	X	X	X	X	30.00	5.02	4.26	4.80	X	1.28	0.29	0.97
Other Services	10.54	17.77	24.14	20.42	9.22	8.57	9.07	8.73	23.90	14.63	7.16	11.61

(Figures in percentage)

Source: 1) District Census Handbook of 1961,1971

2) Census Publication- West Bengal Series part III A & B (i), 1991.

ally decreasing from one census period to another. But in the upper age group e.g. in "C" age bracket it remains more or less constant.

In Table 12 rural female workers per 100 male workers in different industrial category and non-working group are given.

Arrangement was made on the basis of age bracket followed in Table 11. From the table it can be seen that females of "A" age bracket are more or less heavily engaged in different activities in comparison to other age brackets. This is true in case of all censuses. Obviously, in this age group per 100 male non-workers, female non-workers are less in number. This is a contributing factor for low level of literacy and high dropout of girl students from different classes of schools. With the increase in age, numbers of female non-worker go berserk. Ratio of non-workers is the lowest in 0-14 age group. For ordinary job like agricultural labour, the most favoured age bracket is "B" i.e. the age group 15-34 or 15-39. In household industry contribution of females of 0-14 age group is significant. In manufacturing, engagement of 0.14 age group gradually declines from the ever highest of 67.56 percent in 1961 to 26.06 percent in 1981. This may be due to preference for male workers to female workers. Though women are now undertaking different activities of tertiary sectors, but their share in workforce of this sector is not increasing considerably over the period of 1961-1981. From the Table it can be inferred that mostly the span of working life of rural females is limited to the age group 5-39 and contract rapidly with the increase in their ages. More non-working females belong to age bracket of 35-59 or 40-59 of the productive age group 15-59. Therefore ratio of women participants per 100 male participants is low in all industrial category; only of non-working women participants exceed their male counterparts.

CONCLUSION

There is no doubt that employment holds the key to improvement in status. Higher participation in work implies more income and better well-being. But till now, the scope of gainful employment in favour of women is very much limited. It is not that they are not willing to work outside for remuneration, rather it is a fact that they are forced to remain within the four walls of their households for unpaid household management. Until and unless outlook is changed both within their families and society at large, women have to bear the burden of unpaid services.

However, Eighth Five Year Plan emphasised especially empowerment of women. The objective is to make women equal partners and participants in development programmes, not just as beneficiaries of different schemes of development. In order to strengthen the grass roots level women's organizations and groups, promoting participation of women in grass-roots level institutions as envisaged in the 72nd and 73rd Constitutional Amendments and enhancing access of women to education, training, credit and productive and sustained employment opportunities are a few other elements of the approach to empowerment of women (Batra, *op.cit.*,10). But many a time it has been found that the things are lying at the stage of passing resolutions and setting up of Committees and Commissions only, which will not improve the status of women workforce in the countryside until and unless there is strong special and concentrated actions. They must not be treated at par with urban women. With a view to portraying miseries and helplessness of rural women the present study concentrates on rural women and that too in a not so developed district of West Bengal.

REFERENCES

Assam Tribune, January 14, 2002.

Batra, S.L. *Employment for Women* (New Delhi: Har Anand Publications), 1996, pp.10,16,17.

Census of India, Series 23(West Bengal), Part III A & B, 1981. (i) : Govt. of India Publication, p. 23.

District Census Handbook, Birbhum, 1961: p. 66

Human Development Report, UNDP, 1995.

Instruction to Enumerators, 1991 Census, Govt. of India Publication; p. 33

Swaminathan, M.S. 'Intensive Farming: Rational of Integrated System', in *Survey of India Agriculture*, The Hindu Publication, 1995, P.Q.

III

Status of Female-Headed Household

Status problem of female-headed households is gradually becoming the topic of great concern in the context of the women development. It is widely accepted that development of family, especially the economic development in a male dominated society is largely dependent on male members, which automatically benefit the female partners of the family. Till the Sixth Five Year Plan it was not felt necessary to assist women separately for betterment of families. Only at the time of extending assistance to women members the cases of women headed families came to the fore. In this circumstances oppressed women community are the most sufferers when the women have to be the family heads by virtue of natural causes like death of male head (widow) or unnatural cause like divorce, separation (having no legal sanctity), including male migration, matrilineal, female assertiveness and male delinquency, amongst others (Dreze, 1990:1). The literature on Female-Headed households provides an obvious starting point since female heads in rural India are often found to include a very large proportion of widows, (ISST, 1984, Visaria, 1980: 189-223; Raj and Ranadive, 1984; Parthasarathy, 1982; Bhave, 1983, Gulati, 1983: 24-31; 1987: EPW 41-46; Visaria and Visaria, 1985; Agarwal, 1986: 13;Kumari, 1986; 1988a; 1988b; 1988c; 1989; Jetly, 1987; EPW, 1987, 47-53; Krishnakumari, 1987; Chatterjee, 1988; ILO, 1988; Josheph and Pye 1988, Menchar, 1988; Singh; :1988 Singh and Kelles-Viitanen, 1988). These female-headed households experience uncertainty and miseries. In India, however, there is no reliable statistics to have a concrete idea about the female-headed households. Only in 1990 National Sample Survey Organisation, in its report on the 43rd round of employment and unemployment survey, incorporated some statistics relating to Female-Headed Household (FHH). Keeping in mind the importance of preparing a profile of FHH and at the same time in consideration of lack of sufficient relevant data on this theme, this present work has been organized in Nanoor block of the District Birhum in the State of West Bengal.

Block Nanoor was selected mainly for the mixed character of its population and secondly for its considerable level of development in comparison to other blocks of the district. For this purpose ten villages under this block were selected randomly. All families of these ten villages were surveyed through a pre-structured questionnaire and interview method. Selected villages are thus Santoshpur, Berugram, Pakurhans, Kumira, Sakulipur, Chitgram, Ranipur, Ukrundi, Ratanpur and Chandidasnanoor (the head quarter of Nanoor block).

OBJECTIVES

The present study was undertaken with the following objectives:

1. To ascertain the operational existence of Female-Headed household in comparison to the total household of these villages.
2. To draw a socio-economic profile of Female-Headed Households (FHH)
3. To have an idea about the asset holding (including land) of Female-Headed Households.
4. To clarify Rural Female-Headed household on the basis of their per annum income so as to reveal the poverty scenario within these families, and
5. To get their options for various self-employment schemes with a view to alleviating poverty barrier.

METHODOLOGY

In the socio-economic profile, size of FHHs, sex ratio within these families, caste composition, literacy level, dependency ratio and occupational status of families are studied and presented. At the time of studying asset ownership pattern of FHHs, both agricultural and non-agriculture assets are taken into account. Agricultural assets are further classified into three components namely, land, animal assets and agricultural implements. Only quantum of cultivable land is covered for the study. In calculating per annum income of families, incomes from all sources are added up. Per annum income thus calculated for FHHs on the basis of Government of India classification of income, i.e., Rs.0 - 2,265/- (destitute), Rs. 2,266 - 3, 500/- (very very poor), Rs.3, 500 - 5,000/- (very poor) and Rs.5,001 - 6, 400/ - (poor) is followed here. Families having per annum income of Rs.6,400/- are identified as poor. Options for self-employment schemes mean the families' willingness to adopt schemes under IRDP. In this study information on the names of schemes and quantum of investment required are collected.

DISCUSSION OF STUDY RESULTS

The Operational Existence of Female-Headed Households (FHH)

Out of 2367 households (according to 1981 Census) residing in ten villages, women exclusively head 178 i.e., 7.52 per cent families are Female-Headed.(see Table 1 below):

Table 1
Extent of Female-Headed Households

Sl.No.	*Village Name*	*No. of total households*	*No. of FHH*	*Percentage*
1.	Santoshpur	98	5	5.10
2.	Berugram	145	10	6.89
3.	Pakurhans	497	43	8.65
4.	Kumira	122	11	9.01

5.	Sakulipur	168	17	10.11
6.	Chitgram	107	14	13.08
7.	Ranipur	124	9	7.25
8.	Ukrundi	104	6	5.76
9.	Ratanpur	85	10	11.76
10.	Ch. Nanoor	917	53	5.78
	Total	2367	178	7.52

From a report of 43rd round of NSSO at all India level in 1987-88 10.4 per cent families are Female-Headed. During that period in WB, 9% rural existence of village-wise are FHH. From this Table it can be seen that in Chitgram village 13.08 per cent of total households are Female-Headed.

If Table 1 is reduced to the following form, it can be visualized that in 7 villages the FHH are more than 2 per cent (all India estimate).

Percentage of FHH	*Number of Village*
Above 5 to 6	3
Above 6 to 8	2
Above 8 to 10	2
Above 10 to 12	2
Above 12	1

Household Formation

For making comparative statements, family sizes of all households of villages are presented in Table 2 (a).

Average family size of FHH as calculated in the present study is 3.17. Average size of all families taken together is 5.50, i.e. more than double (73.50 per cent) of average size of FHH. But in FHH there is preponderance of female members. In 564 members of all FHH, 59.92% are female while of 13037 members of all families of the villages, 49.64 per cent are female.

Table 2 (a)
Sex ratio of FHH and AH

Sl.No.	Village Name	No. of household Male	Female	Total	FHH Male	Female	Total	Percentage AH	FHH
1.	Santoshpur	277	254	531	15	12	27	5.41	5.40
2.	Berugram	360	366	726.	15	21	36	5.00	3.60
3.	Pakurhans	1395	1364	2759	31	67	98	5.55	2.28
4.	Kumira	352	379	731	11	21	32	5.99	2.90
5.	Sakulipur	460	483	943	17	38	55	5.61	3.23
6.	Chitgram	318	317	635	22	20	42	5.93	3.00
7.	Ranipur	367	360	727	12	14	26	5.86	2.89
8.	Ukrundi	337	349	686	13	11	24	6.60	4.00
9.	Ratanpur	225	232	457	23	22	45	5.37	4.50
10.	Ch. Nanoor	2470	2372	4842	67	112	179	5.28	3.37
	Over all Total	6561	6476	13037	226	338	564	5.50	3.17

AH= All Households. FHH=Female-Headed Households

The villages with sex ratio in FHH and all households are presented in Table 2 (b) below:

Table 2 (b)
Sex ratio of FHH and AH

Sl. No.	Village Name	AH	FHH
1.	Santoshpur	917	800
2.	Berugram	1016	1400
3.	Pakuhans	978	2161
4.	Kumira	1076	1909
5.	Sakulipur	1050	2235
6.	Chitgram	996	909
7.	Ranipur	980	1166
8.	Ukrundi	1035	846
9.	Ratanpur	1031	956
10.	Ch. Nanoor	960	1617
	Over all Total	987	1495

As per the Table above in Sakulipur village sex ratio is as high as 2235. Overall FHH, sex ratio was found to be 1495, which is 51.47 per cent higher than sex ratio (987) of all households taken together. Block sex ratio on the basis of 1981 census is 983 and that of the district Birbhum is 966. Therefore, in FHH, on the one hand, there exists preponderance of female members, and on the other, the family size is small. In the prevailing social structure and belief system the position of females is more disadvantageous in already jeopardised Female-Headed Households.

According to the community-wise break up (Table 2 (c)) it can be seen that among the Muslim families, the number of family members are more.

Table 2 (c)

Community wise Distribution of Female-Headed Families on the basis of number of Family Member

Community	*Number of Family members*					
	1	*2-4*	*5-7*	*8-10*	*More than 10*	*Total*
Scheduled Caste	13	51	8	—	—	72
Scheduled Tribe	—	6	1	—	—	7
Muslim	2	28	19	1	—	50
Upper Hindu Caste	9	25	14	1	—	49
Total	24	110	42	2	—	178

For example, whereas in scheduled castes community 13 families have one member each. In case of Muslim FHH there are two such families. Further, in Muslim community in 38 per cent families it is 11.11 and in upper Hindu castes families the corresponding figure is 28.57 per cent. If these villages are taken together, then 61.80 per cent female-headed families have family size in the range of 2-4 members. 23.60 per cent FHH have 5-7 members family size, while in the case of 13.48 per cent all the families are single headed.

Caste Breakup of FHH

In Table (3) female-headed households of the village are distributed over four groups viz. scheduled castes, scheduled tribes, Muslim and upper Hindu caste.

Table 3
Caste Breakup of Female-Headed Households (FHH)

Sl.No.	*Village Name*	*Total FHH*	*SC*	*ST*	*Muslim Community*	*Upper Hindu Caste*
1.	Santoshpur	5	—	—	5	—
2.	Berugram	10	2	—	8	—
3.	Pakurhans	43	24	3	3	13
4.	Kumira	11	3	1	1	6
5.	Sakulipur	17	—	—	11	6
6.	Chitgram	14	11	—	—	3
7.	Ranipur	9	7	—	—	—
8.	Ukrundi	6	5	—	—	1
9.	Ratanpur	10	3	2	5	—
10.	Ch. Nanoor	53	17	1	16	19
	Total	178	72 (40.45)	7 (3.93)	50 (28.09)	49 (27.53)

Figure under parenthesis denotes percentage of the individual caste to the total.

All villages taken together, 40.45 per cent FHHs belong to SC community and the rest 27.53 per cent are upper Hindu caste. In Chandidas Nanoor Village FHHs are more or less evenly distributed over SC, Muslim and general castes. In Berugram and Sakulipur villages, Berugram's share of Muslim FHH is 80 per cent while in case of the second one it is 64.70 per cent. In Muslim families there are more female members than in other communities. Even if we consider all households figure for sex ratio, in case of Sakulipur and Berugram it is more than overall sex ratio of ten villages.

Literacy Status

Out of the total 564 members of FHHs only 80 are literate in the sense that they can write names only is shown in Table 4 (a). Majority of them have no formal education.

Table 4 (a)
Literacy Status of Female-Headed Households (FHH)

Sl.No.	*Village Name*	*Member of FHH*			*No. of literate ember*			*Literate Percentage*
		Male	*Female*	*Total*	*Male*	*Female*	*Total*	
1.	Santoshpur	15	12	27	2	—	2	7.40
2.	Berugram	15	21	36	2	—	2	5.55
3.	Pakurhans	31	67	98	7	4	11	11.22
4.	Kumira	11	21	32	9	5	14	43.75
5.	Sakulipur	17	38	55	8	4	12	21.81
6.	Chitgram	22	204	2	3	2	5	11.90
7.	Ranipur	12	14	26	4	2	6	23.07
8.	Ukrundi	13	11	24	1	—	1	4.17
9.	Ratanpur	23	22	45	5	3	8	17.77
10.	Ch. Nanoor	67	112	179	13	9	22	12.29
	Over all Total	226	338	564	54	29	83	15.89

In percentage term only 15.89 per cent members of FHHs are literate while 84.11 per cent are illiterate. If male and female literacy be compared, females are found very much jeopardized; female literacy is to the tune of 8.58 per cent while male literacy is 23.89 per cent. In Kumira village overall literacy level is very high i.e. 43.75 per cent which is highest among all other villages under study. The literacy level of upper Hindu caste of FHHs comes to 51.25 percent. In upper Hindu caste literacy level is 28.47 per cent in comparison to 9.77 for SC, 7.69 for ST and 8.87 per cent for Muslim community. Community wise break - up of literate members of FHHs are given in Table 4 (b).

Table 4 (b)
Community-wise Breakup of literate Members of Female-Headed Households (in members)

Community	*Male Literate*	*Female Literate*	*Male Illiterate*	*Female Illiterate*	*Total*
Scheduled Caste	13	9	74	129	225
Scheduled Tribe	2	—	8	16	26
Muslim	11	4	54	100	169
Upper Hindu Caste	28	13	36	67	144
Total	54	26	172	312	564

Further, the situation of literacy in FHHs can be apprehended from the following structure:

	Male Literacy (in percent)	*Female Literacy (in percent)*
FHH	23.89	8.58
All Households of villages under study	41.33	25.32
block	43.11	27.38

Occupational Status and Earning Members of FHH

Table 5 below presents income-earning activities of the villages under study. Only 46.63 per cent go out for earning and 53.37 per cent are totally engaged in household activities. 25.28 per cent families depend on agriculture sector and sell out their labour for earning. 21.34 per cent are engaged as non-agricultural labourers, 6.75 per cent as rural artisans and 2.80 per cent in various village retail trade and business. Muslim community members usually are not found in considerable number in the job market. Out of 15 families depending on agriculture labour as source of earning, only 2.00, 1.10 and 4.40 per cent from Muslim community. On the other hand, out of

50 Muslim families 41(82 per cent) depend on various household activities like maidservant, contract labour etc. Mostly these works are available within these villages. So in these families mobility among the labourers is hardly seen. They are satisfied with whatever wages are given. For example, wage of maidservant varies from Rs. 20 to Rs. 40 per month. Scheduled Tribe families come out for work against remunerative wages. Out of 7 ST families 5 accepted agriculture labour. In the case of upper Hindu Caste families, members are comparatively enterprising and 5 families adopted self-employment ventures. The self-employment activities of FHHs in the ten villages are strikingly limited (see Table 5 below for further details).

Table 5
Occupational Status of Female-Headed Households

Type of Occupation	*SC*	*ST*	*Muslim Community*	*Upper Hindu Caste*	*Total*
Household Activities	34	—	41	20	95
Agricultural Labour	25	5	2	13	45
Labour	9	2	7	3	21
Rural Artisan	4	—	—	8	12
Service-Business	—	—	—	5	5
Total	72	7	50	49	178

In FHHs out of 564 members 230 earn for their families i.e. 40.78 per cent members are self-earning members and 59.22 per cent membe. ̦ are non-earning. pendency ratio for all FHHs of ten villages is calculated at 2.45. Of 226 male members 49.11 per cent earn for their families while of 338 female members, only 35.20 per cent earn for their families. In ten villages under study, of 6476 female members only 263 (4.06 per cent) are working members. Of working females 110, i.e. 45.25 per cent belong to FHHs (see Table 6).

Table 6
Earning Members of Female-Headed Households

Sl.No.	Village Name	Total Members			Earning Member			Dependency Ratio
		Male	Female	Total	Male	Female	Total	
1.	Santoshpur	15	12	21	3	4	7	3.86
2.	Berugram	15	21	36	5	7	12	3.00
3.	Pakurhans	31	67	98	21	23	44	2.22
4.	Kumira	11	21	32	6	5	11	2.90
5.	Sakulipur	17	38	55	9	11	20	2.75
6.	Chitgram	22	20	42	11	10	21	2.00
7.	Ranipur	12	14	26	5	6	11	2.36
8.	Ukrundi	13	11	24	4	3	7	3.43
9.	Ratanpur	23	22	45	8	9	17	2.46
10.	Ch. Nanoor	67	112	179	39	41	80	2.23
	Over all Total	226	338	564	111	119	230	2.45

This implies that though most of the women of the villages remain non-workers, women of FHH undertake some jobs for sustenance of their families. It should be stressed that the focus of this Table is on the "income aspect" of employment rather than on either the "production aspect" or the "reorganization aspects". Our concern here is with the activities of FHHs to earn income in cash or kind that gives them an independent command over commodities through market exchange. This is because these activities enhance their economic independence and bargaining power in a way that simply does not apply to, say child minding, cooking or fetching water from the point of view of the household economy. This is no prc f to say that a clear-cut line be drawn between "income causing" and other economic activities as the information, presented in this Table has limitations, largely reflecting the general difficulties that effect occupational statistics (especially when it comes to female employment). In spite of these limitations, a number of features of occupational patterns in these villages are worth noting.

Assets of FHHs

In studying the asset holding pattern of Female-Headed Households, information on cultivable land holding, animal assets like milch cow, goats, pigs etc., agricultural implements like spade, sickle, cuttery, sprayer, duster etc., and non-agricultural implements is collected and presented in table 7 (a) to Table 8 (c). Most of the Female-Headed families have no cultivable land here, 60.11 per cent have no land for cultivation. In Table 7 (a) FHHs are distributed on the basis of landholding.

Table 7 (a)

Landholding (in acres) pattern of FHH

Sl.No.	*Village Name*	*0.0*	*Up to 0.33*	*Above 0.33 to 1.00*	*Above 1.00 to 2.50*	*Above 2.50 to 5.00*
1.	Santoshpur	4	1	—	—	—
2.	Berugram	6	2	2	—	—
3.	Pakurhans	26	8	5	3	1
4.	Kumira	4	2	4	1	—
5.	Sakulipur	12	3	2	—	—
6.	Chitgram	9	4	1	—	—
7.	Ranipur	3	2	1	2	1
8.	Ukrundi	2	2	1	1	—
9.	Ratanpur	2	2	4	2	—
10.	Ch. Nanoor	39	8	5	1	—
	Over all Total	107	34	25	10	2

Only 2 families belonging to upper Hindu caste have landholding in the range of 2.50 acres to 5 acres, 19.10 per cent families have landholding to the extent of 1 Bigha, i.e. 0.33 acres. Of the families having no land at all 32.71 per cent belong to the scheduled caste and of 7 tribal families none have land at all.

In Table 7(b) community wise – break - up of landholding pattern reflects that 61.11 per cent scheduled caste families and 70 per cent Muslim families have no land asset (see Table 7 (b)) below:

Table 7 (b)
Community - wise Breakup of Land-holdings (in acres) of FHH

Caste	*Nil 0.33*	*Upto 0.33 to 1.00*	*Above 0.33 to 1.00*	*Above 1.00 to 2.50*	*Above 2.50 to 5.00*	*Total*
Scheduled Caste	44	16	9	3	—	72
Scheduled Tribe	7	—	—	—	—	7
Muslim	35	10	5	—	—	50
Upper Hindu Caste	21	8	12	6	2	49
Total	107	34	26	9	2	178

Barring land, assets are divided into three categories such as animal assets, agricultural implements and non-agricultural assets. No female-headed family possesses pump set, sprayers and dusters. The question of possessing a tractor does not arise at all.

Mostly they are with one or two sickles, spades, some *cuttery*, plough etc. Here, non-agricultural assets imply bicycle, cycle van and handloom see, Table 8 (a).

From Table 8 (c) it can be visualised that in total assets of FHH the share of non-agricultural assets is only 2.97 per cent, which signifies very primitive mode of activities. Traditional agricultural implements occupy 75.09 per cent of total assets. Animal assets mainly comprising goats, pigs and few poultry birds of indigenous variety account for 21.93 per cent of total

Table 8 (a)
Assets Holding Patern of FHH

Sl.No.	Village Name	Animal assets	Agricultural implements	Non-assets agricultural	Total
1.	Santoshpur	—	4	—	4
2.	Berugram	2	17	—	19
3.	Pakurhans	14	45	2	61
4.	Kumira	—	19	—	19
5.	Sakulipur	3	14	—	17
6.	Chitgram	4	16	—	20
7.	Ranipur	2	11	—	13
8.	Ukrundi	3	9	—	12
9.	Ratanpur	6	18	—	24
10.	Ch. Nanoor	25	49	6	80
	Over all Total	59 (21.93)	202 (75.09)	8 (2.97)	269

(Figure under Parenthesis indicates percentage share of the total assets)

assets. Only a few families in Chandidas Nanoor Village possess two milch cows each and that too of indigenous variety. In the total assets out of the villages, the share of FHH is 8.90

Table 8 (b)
Community-wise Breakup of Assets of FHH

Caste	Animal Assets	Agricultural implements	Non-agricultural assets	Total
Scheduled Caste	26	96	2	124
Scheduled Tribe	2	3	—	5
Muslim	12	64	3	79
Upper Hindu Caste	19	39	3	61
Total	59	202	8	269

per cent (269 of FHH against 3020 of all household). The share of women - headed Families in total animal assets of the village is 9.82 per cent, while their share in agricultural implements and non-agricultural implements is 8.74 and 7.33 per cent respectively. Table 8 (b) gives the community-wise breakup of assets, where the share of animal assets (44.06 per cent) is the greatest among the SC families followed by the share (32.20 per cent) of upper Hindu caste families.

In this category the share of Muslim families is only 20.33 per cent. Table 8 (c) below gives the picture about the number of Female-Headed Families who are not having assets at all.

Table 8 (c)

Community - wise Breakup of Families having no Assets

Sl. No.	*Village Name*	*No. of FHH*	*No. of FHH having no assets*	*Community*			
				SC	*ST*	*Muslim*	*Upper Hindu Caste*
1.	Santoshpur	5	3	—	—	3	—
2.	Berugram	10	2	—	—	2	—
3.	Pakurhans	43	7	—	—	—	7
4.	Kumira	11	4	—	1	1	2
5.	Sakulipur	17	11	—	—	7	4
6.	Chitgram	14	3	3	—	—	—
7.	Ranipur	9	2	1	—	—	—
8.	Ukrundi	6	—	—	—	—	—
9.	Ratanpur	10	3	3	—	—	—
10.	Ch. Nanoor	53	16	1	—	4	11
	Over all Total	178	51	8	1	17	25

34 per cent families of Muslim community and 51.02 per cent upper Hindu caste families have no assets at all and in scheduled caste families only 11.11 per cent have no assets. In Santoshpur and Sakulipur village respectively 60 and 63.63 per

cent Muslim families respectively have no assets at all. In Chandidas - Nanoor village about 58 percent female-headed families have no assets at all.

Income of FHHs

From the occupational status of Female-Headed Households it is very much clear that they depend largely on traditional sources of earning. For obvious reasons their earnings are very meager. It can be seen from the Table 9 that 43.25 per cent of FHHs are in destitute income group whereas 41.78 per cent of all families have income more than Rs. 6400/- per annum (poverty line).

Table 9
Distribution of FHH by per annum Income vis-a-vis All Households

Range of Income	*Number of households*		*Percentage*	
(in Rupees)	*Female-Headed*	*AH*	*FHH*	*AH*
0-2265	77	537	43.25	22.68
2266-3500	65	383	36.52	16.18
3501-5000	25	252	14.04	14.92
5001-6400	8	105	4.50	4.44
Above 6400	3	989	1.69	41.78
Total	178	2367	100.00	100.00

Again 79.77 per cent of FHHs are in the category of destitute and very very poor whereas only 38.86 per cent of total families are in these two lowest groups.

From community-wise breakup of FHHs (Table 10) on the basis of their yearly income, it can be seen that 64 per cent Muslim families are in the income range of Rs.0-2265.

The condition of ST families is also very serious as of 7 families, 6 families belong to this group. 36.11 per cent of SC

Table 10
Community - wise Distribution of FHH vis-a-vis Income

Per annum Income (in Rupees)	*SC*	*ST*	*Muslim Community*	*Upper Hindu Caste*	*Total*
0-2265	26	6	32	13	77
2266-3500	32	1	11	21	65
3501-5000	12	—	7	6	25
5001-6400	2	—	—	6	8
Above 6400	—	—	—	3	3
Total	72	7	50	49	178

and 26.53 per cent of upper Hindu caste families are also in this lowest income group. Economically, upper Hindu caste female-headed families are comparatively better placed in relation to SC, ST and Muslim families.

Option For Self-Employment Scheme

Considering the stark poverty situation within FHH, options were taken from the head of the household in respect of self-employment schemes to be provided under Integrated Rural Development Programme. 35.68 per cent of respondents opted for rice processing, 1/.84 per cent for muri-making, 24.86 per cent for animal husbandry schemes, 10.32 per cent for goat rearing, 10.32 per cent for house dairy and 4.22 per cent for calf raising, 2.82 per cent for bidi rolling and 11.80 per cent for business sector activities.

Detailed scheme-wise distribution is given in Table 11 above, where 178 families opted for 213 schemes. Here also most of the families do not want a package of schemes (in spite of provision in the programme) mainly for avoiding loan burden.

Table 11
Scheme-wise Distribution of Female-Headed Households

Sl.No.	*Preferred Scheme-wise*	*No. of Scheme*	*Percentage*
1.	Rice Processing	76	35.68
2.	Muri Making	38	17.84
3.	Badi Making	7	3.29
4.	Bidi Rolling	6	2.82
5.	Weaving	2	0.94
6.	Calf Rearing	9	4.22
7.	Goat Rearing	22	10.32
8.	House Dairy	22	10.32
9.	Backyard Poultry	4	1.88
10.	Sheep Rearing	1	0.47
11.	Retail Business	15	7.04
12.	Grocery	2	0.94
13.	Stationery	1	0.47
14.	Bullock-Cart	4	1.88
15.	Cycle Repairing	1	0.47
16.	Vegetable vending	3	1.42
	Total	213	100.00

As revealed in the course of field study, these families, mostly due to ignorance, expressed very lukewarm attitude towards adopt more schemes for betterment of their families. Not only this, female - headed families are very much shy in respect of availing innovative schemes. They prefer traditional schemes with lower scheme value. This is mainly due to their deplorable economic conditions, which influence them to avoid activities involving risk and uncertainity.

CONCLUSION AND SUGGESTIONS

In fact members of Female-Headed Households live in a closed circuit of economic deprivations, illiteracy and lack of skill of interaction between each other. Until and unless external intervention is made it is unlikely that their conditions will ever change. Even after introduction of massive poverty alleviation programmes like Integrated Rural Development Programme, the conditions of these families did not improve much. The main reason is that in practice, women of male-headed families are preferred more at the time of selection of beneficiaries because of their secured position. Not a single out of 178 families received assistance under IRDP within twelve years of its operation. The cause is vulnerability of Female-Headed Household. Rural Development functionaries including Bank people often feel that these families may not run the scheme efficiently and consequently may not be able to repay Bank dues. It is suggested to reserve 5 to 10 per cent allocations of IRDP out of 40 per cent already specified for women beneficiaries. In TRYSEM scheme and JRY also this short of specification need to be made to help Female-Headed families to get rid of wretched conditions. Lastly, it needs to be mentioned that only economic measures alone cannot eliminate all the evils; these measures must be and should be supplemented by social actions also for alleviating deprivation of female-headed households.

REFERENCES

Agarwal, B., "Women Poverty and Agricultural Growth in India", *Journal of Peasant Studies*, 1986.

———, "Tribal Matriliny in Transition", mimeo, Institute of Economic Growth, Delhi, 1989.

Bhave, S., "Women Headed Households in India, A micro Study from an Indian Slum", paper presented at the Expert Group Meeting on forward-looking strategies for the advancement of women, *ESCAP*, Bangkok, December, 1983.

Chatterjee, S., "Rise in Female-Headed Families", in *The Indian Women Search for an Identity*, New Delhi: Vikda, 1988.

Dreze, Jean, *Widows in Rural India*, Discussion Paper, Series No. 26, *STICERD*, London School of Economics, August, 1990.

Gulati, L., "Male migration to the Middle East and the Impact on the Family", *Economic and Political Weekly*, December 24-31, 1983.

———, "Coping with Male Migration", *Economic and Political Weekly*, 22 (44): WS 41-46, 1987.

Institute of Social Studies Trust, "India's Female-Headed Households", report submitted to the *ILO*, Geneva, 1984.

ILO, "Female-Headed Households and the Development of guidelines for their Participation in Development," *Proceedings of a National Workshop* held in Delhi, April, 1984.

Jetley, S., "Migration and Women-Headed Households in Uttar Pradesh", paper presented at the First Regional Conference on Women's Decade and Public Policy, ANDMM College, Kamrup. n.d.

———, "Impact of Male Migration on Rural Females", *Economic and Political Weekly*, 1987, 22 (44), WS 47-53.

Joseph, R.M. and Pye, E.A., "Identifying the Assistance needs of Female-Headed Households in Asia", paper presented at the 12th Congress of the International Union of Anthrological and Ethnological Sciences, Zagreb, July 1988.

Krishna Kumari, N.S., *Status of Single Women in India*, Delhi. Uppal, 1987.

Kumari, R., *Rural Female-Headed Households: Need for Policy Intervenstion*, New Delhi: Centre for Social Research, 1986.

———, "Female-Headed Households: Conceptual and Definitional Problems", paper presented at National Workshop on Female-Headed Households and the Development of guidelines for their participation in Development, New Delhi, April 1988.

———, *Rural Women Headed Households in North India*, Paper presented at the 12th Congress of the International Union of Anthological and Ethnological Sciences, Zagreb, July 24-31, 1988.

———, *Women Headed Households in India*, New Delhi: Radiant Publishers, 1989.

Mencher, J.P., "Female- Headed/Female Supported Households in India: who are they and What Survival Strategies are Possible for them?" paper presented at the 12th Congress of the International Union of Anthropological and Ethnological Sciences, Zagreb, July 24-31, 1988.

Parthasarathy, G., "Rural Poverty and Female Heads of Households: Need for quantitative Analysis", paper presented at Technical Seminar on Women's Work and Employment, Institute of Social Studies Trust, New Delhi, April 9-11, 1982.

Raj, M.K; and Ranadive, J., "The Rural Female Heads of Households: Hidden from View", in Manohar, M.(ed), *Women Status and Development in India*, 1984.

Singh, A., "Female-Headed Households: An Overview of the Concept and its application to poverty Alleviation", paper presented at the National Workshop on Female-Headed Households and the Development guidelines for their participation in Development, New Delhi, April 26-28, 1988.

Singh, A.M. and Velles-Viitamen, A.O., "Defining and Targeting Female-Headed –Households for Development Assistance in South Asia", paper presented at the 12th Congress of the International Union of Anthropological and Ethnological Sciences, Zegreb, July 24-31, 1988.

Visaria, P., "Poverty and Living Standards in Asia", *Population and Development Review*, 1980 6 (2) 189-223.

Visaria, P. and Visaria, L., "Indian Households with Female Heads: Their incidence, characteristics and levels of living", in Jain and Banerjee (eds.), *Tyranny of the Household*, New Delhi: Vikas, 1985.

IV

Policies and Programmes Related To Women

Since the inception of the plan era in 1951 (when the First Five Year Plan was launched) thrust has been given on Development of Women. But till 1971 the thrust was mainly on welfare aspect of women and the economic front was not adequately taken into consideration. It is the publication of the report of the Committee on Status of Women in 1974 (set up by Govt. of India in 1971) and the declaration by United Nations to observe 1975 as International Women's Year, that has caused a lot of changes in the focal points of women development. It has been widely recognized that despite being half of the population of the society, the women did not receive adequate attention in the programmes launched for development of the economy. The Sixth Five Year Plan for the first time in the history of planning in India, included a chapter on 'Women and Child Development' and amply recognised that the women were deprived of the fruits of development to a great extent. For bringing women to the main stream of development, the Sixth Plan recommended a list of programmes exclusively for women. One such programme was Development of Women and Children in Rural Areas (DWCRA)(Prasad, 1996:1-2; Reddy and Renuka, 1994). This programme was started in the year 1982-83 as a sub-scheme of Integrated Rural Development Programme (IRDP). The programme was so named because it is widely believed that with the development of mothers, development of children also comes simultaneously and this two fold development is inseparable-one influences the other. In general the basic objective of the programme is to enable poor rural women to get organised into small groups with the purpose of understanding and analysing their existing situations, thereby finding out solutions to their miseries. The earlier programme designed for development of women had their main focus on the domestic responsibilities of women which means that women were to be educated in larger number because they would serve their families in a better way, take care of their children more hygienically. These programmes did not recognize that women had a lot to contribute not only to their families but also to the economy of the country as a whole. But this recognition came only after the report of the Committee on Status of Women, and then it has gained strength from year to year. In DWCRA also, provision has been made for income generating activities of women.

Specifically DWCRA aims at:

— improving the status and quality of life of poor rural women and their children;
— enabling rural women to improve their earning capacity through engagements in income generating activities;
— improving the impact of on-going development programmes in rural areas through their integration and convergence;
— organising women so that they may be involved in planning and implementing the programmes directly benefiting them;
— self-subsistence even after help is withdrawn.

All these taken together are expected to lead to their empowerment and enhancement of their status. DWCRA has some unique features in comparison to other Government programmes like IRDP, JRY and any other programmes. It may be noted that while most of the programmes are family based, DWCRA is group oriented. Secondly, most of the programmes depend totally on the assistance from the government and once the assistance is withdrawn the programme has to be abandoned. But in DWCRA emphasis is also placed on self-reliance of the group. Initially, the government may give some grant but that grant is for one time – the group has to manage their activities with this fund. Thirdly, in DWCRA, groups function independently and take decisions themselves- their activities are based on awareness and stimulation for self - help. But in the case of other programmes and schemes, institutional arrangements are made for running them. Fourthly, the name of the programme indicates that it is meant for women and children residing in rural areas; thus the target group is specific. In other programmes, for example IRDP, or JRY or Ceiling Surplus Land Distribution, the whole population living below the poverty line is taken as the target group. With this introduction of the above programme, the present study has been taken up to narrate the progress of DWCRA since its inception. Though at the all India level the programme has been started since 1982-83 as a pilot project in 50 districts of the country with the assistance from UNICEF, in West Bengal the programme was launched only in the year 1983-84.

The objectives of taking up this study are as follows:

i) To visualize the extent of coverage of the programme;
ii) To overview the utilization pattern of revolving funds given to groups for carrying out their income generating activities;
iii) To study how far DWCRA has been linked up with other on-going poverty alleviation programmes like IRDP and TRYSEM; and;
iv) To review the infrastructure provisions behind the programme.

However, the study is based on the secondary source of data and covers all the districts of the state.

The Study

In West Bengal, the programme made its beginning in the year 1983-84. Two districts were taken up in the first year of the programme, namely, Bankura and Purulia, because economically both the districts were very poor. Therefore, in the year1986-87, Jalpaiguri was brought under the programme, and in the next three years the programme was extended to South 24 Parganas, North 24 Parganas and Hooghly districts respectively. In the first year of the Eight Plan, Birbhum and Malda were brought within the map of DWCRA, and in the year 1984-85 the programme was extended to all the remaining districts of the state. The year-wise coverage of the districts is presented in the Table below:

Table 1
Year-wise Coverage of Districts under DWCRA

Year	*Name of District (S) Covered*
1983-84	Bankura, Purulia
1986-87	Jalpaiguri
1987-88	South 24 Parganas
1988-89	North 24 Paraganas
1989-90	Hooghly
1991-92	Burdwan, Midnapur
1992-93	Birbhum, Malda
1993-94	Murshidabad and hill areas of Darjeeling
1994-95	Siliguri sub division of Darjeeling District, Coach Behar, Uttar Dinajpur and Dokshin Dinajpur, Howrah and Nadia.

Source: Rural Development Department, Govt. of West Bengal, 1996.

Coverage of the Programme

Though in all the districts of the state, DWCRA was extended, but only 323 blocks out of 341 in the state could be covered under the programme; under percentage term this is 73.90 percent of the total blocks (see Table 2). In Table 2, coverage of blocks under DWCRA vis-à-vis total number of blocks in the district are presented. This table shows how far it became possible to bring DWCRA to the doorstep of the villagers for garnering its benefits. More block coverage implies that the programme is gaining ground at the grass root level.

Table 2
Year-wise Coverage of Blocks under DWCRA

Name of District	*Total no. of Blocks in the Districts*	*No. of Blocks covered*	*Percentage coverage*
Coach Behar	12	12	100.00
Jalpaiguri	13	13	100.00
Darjeeling	12	12	100.00
Uttar Dinajpur	9	9	100.00
Dakshin Dinajpur	7	7	100.00
Malda	15	15	100.00
Murshidabad	26	20	76.92
Nadia	17	14	82.35
North 24 Parganas	22	22	100.00
South 24 Parganas	29	28	96.55
Howrah	14	14	100.00
Hooghly	18	18	100.00
Midnapur	54	54	100.00
Bankura	22	22	100.00
Purulia	20	20	100.00
Burdwan	31	24	77.42
Birbhum	19	19	100.00
West Bengal	341	323	94.72

Source: Panchayat and Rural Development Department, Govt. of West Bengal, 1999.

Out of seventeen districts, in thirteen districts all the blocks were covered under DWCRA. The coverage is the lowest in Burdwan district. But reasons for such low coverage are very difficult to ascertain as number of factors like inept attitude of government functionaries, lack of initiatives on the part of panchayat members etc are acting and inter-acting with each other for making the coverage low. In addition to such attitudinal problems with the functionaries (both officials and non-officials) the non-coverage of blocks is also due to inadequate administration infrastructure. Example of this reason lies in Murshidabad district where the post of Assistant Project Officer (Women Development) at District Rural Development Agency was lying vacant since 1993-94 till the end of 1994-95.

Growth of Groups and Members

DWCRA being a group approach to problems of women, at the beginning of the programme it was decided by the Government of India to form groups of women with 15-20 women of the area. Later on however, the number of women in each group has been reduced to 10-15. In West Bengal, though the programme was launched in the year 1983-84, no groups could be formed in that year mainly due to non-completion of the initial formalities. Thereafter the programme got enough stimulations and a number of Groups grew at a fast pace. In Table 3, growths of DWCRA groups on year-to-year basis are represented.

Since 1992-93 the growth of the groups declined. This decline was due to reduction of target of groups' formation by the Government of India.

The Table, thus, indicates that the rate of growth of the groups has been slowed down year after year. The table 3 (a) is designed to present the growth of membership in DWCRA groups. In DWCRA, women members are taken from the families living below the poverty line (Rs. 11,000. - per annum, according to the Eighth Five-Years Plan). Preferably women are selected from a single village; if not possible then at least

Table 3
Growth of Group Formation in DWCRA

Year	*No. of Groups formed*	*Percentage increase or decrease over the previous year*
1984-85	54	—
1985-86	130	140.74
1986-87	189	102.71
1987-88	238	63.80
1988-89	292	47.79
1989-90	373	38.22
1990-91	386	30.25
1991-92	424	25.51
1992-93	315	15.10
1993-94	340	14.76
1994-95	377	13.75
1995-96	888	135.54
1996-97	1758	67.23
1997-98	1986	33.74
1998-99	1920	(–) 3.32
Total	9670	—

Source : Panchayats and Rural Development Dept. Govt. of West Bengal, 1999

from the adjacent villages so that they can meet regularly and discuss their situations intimately. From the Table it can also be seen that the maximum number of women involvement in DWCRA happened in 1990-91 when 7197 poor women were brought to the fold of DWCRA benefits. In that year average size of a group was 18.64 members. But in the beginning of the Seventh Five Year Plan, the Government of India guidelines reduced the size of group from 15-20 members to 10-15 members. The panchayats that were given the rights to identify women for DWCRA group members preferred to give benefits to more members despite the restrictions on membership in a group.

Table 3 (a)
Growth of Membership in DWCRA

Year	*Total no. of Groups/ Members in the year*	*Percentage Growth of Members over the previous year*	*Average Size of Group*
1984-85	1055	—	19.54
1985-86	2557	242.37	19.67
1986-87	3748	103.76	19.83
1987-88	4142	56.28	17.40
1988-89	6187	53.79	21.19
1989-90	6939	39.23	18.60
1990-91	7197	29.22	18.64
1991-92	7093	22.29	16.73
1992-93	4518	11.67	14.34
1993-94	4572	10.52	13.45
1994-95	5349	11.14	14.19
1995-96	11092	107.36	12.49
1996-97	22087	99.12	14.87
1997-98	26589	20.38	13.39
1998-99	24657	(–) 7.27	12.84
Total	—	—	17.11

Source : Panchayats and Rural Development Dept. Govt. of West Bengal, 1999

From the Table 3(a) it can be noticed that average size of DWCRA group in West Bengal is 17.11 when the size of a group means the number of women in that group. In 1988-89 the size even crossed the Government of India's instruction to limit the size within 20. It is interestingly very high all throughout. Even till now it is more than 15, which is the maximum size limit prescribed by Government of India. The objective behind restricting the size of a DWCRA group is that in small group poor women will participate effectively as the group can be more or less homogeneous. Making the group unnecessary larger cannot deliver the good of the programme, as it is very difficult to build up in large groups.

Table 4

No.of DWCRA Groups and Members: District-wise (till 1998-99)

No. of District	*Total No. of Groups*	*Total No. of Members*	*Average Size of Groups*
Cooch Behar	140	2013	14.38
Jalpaiguri	914	13789	15.08
Darjeeling	516	6749	13.08
Uttar Dinajpur	234	3220	13.76
Dakshin Dinajpur	644	7698	11.95
Malda	415	5550	13.37
Murshidabad	279	3186	11.42
Nadia	225	3230	14.35
North 24 Pargnas	741	10397	14.03
South 24 Pargnas	503	8757	17.41
Howrah	12911	4957	11.58
Hooghly	455	6288	13.82
Midnapur	537	7914	14.74
Bankura	870	14638	16.82
Purulia	1163	19682	16.92
Burdwan	320	4264	13.32
Birbhum	423	4740	11.20
Total	9670	137072	14.17

Source : Panchayats and Rural Development Dept. Govt. of West Bengal, 1999

Since 1994-95 five more districts and Siliguri Sub-division of Darjeeling district were brought within the map of DWCRA. All the districts of the state having rural areas are thus covered by the programme for women and child development. District-wise number of groups and members covered are shown in Table-4 wherefrom district-wise distribution of group size and members may be available.

In Cooch Behar and Dakshin Dinajpur District it was not possible to organize women groups under DWCRA till the end of the year 1994-95. In Purulia District neither new groups were formed nor any increase in the membership was registered. The average size of the group (i.e., the number of members per group) varies from district to district-it is as low as 11.75 in Birbhum and as high as 19.18 in Bankura. Though the Government of India, from the Seventh Five-year Plan restricted the size of the groups to 10-15 members, in a number of districts where DWCRA was introduced during the Seventh Plan this norm was flouted. For example, Jalpaiguri where DWCRA was launched in the year 1986-87 (the second year of the Seventh Plan), the average size of the groups at the end of 1994-95 became 16-62. Again in South 24 Parganas the size is larger in comparison to North Parganas. Out of the seventeen districts two districts where DWCRA is yet to start functioning. Hence, they were left for analysis purpose, then in seven districts the norm of 10-15 members group size is followed at the time of formation of the groups and in the remaining eight districts, this norm was not followed, because the Panchayats and Government officials want to give benefits, whatever it may be, to more number of women. In the process qualitative aspects of the programme are being damaged.

Revolving Fund

For pursuing economic activities each group of women under DWCRA is given lump sum grant of Rs. 15,000 as a revolving fund. The equal shares from the Government of India, State Government and UNICEF constitute this fund. The revolving fund has now increased from Rs. 15,000/- to Rs.

25,000/- per group since last 1996. UNICEF's support of fund was withdrawn from Jan 1st 1996. The fund is so called because this fund is never exhausted- once it is lent out to members and again the members repay it, so that total amount of fund remains intact. According to the Government of India's manual, the group may use the revolving fund amount for the following purposes:

- — Honorarium to group organizer at the rate of Rs.50/-per month for a period of one year.
- — One time expenditure not exceeding Rs. 500/- to meet traveling allowances of group members for visiting banks, officers etc.
- — One time expenditure for creating childcare facilities.
- — Purchasing raw materials and marketing products of the group.
- — Infrastructure support for income generating activities and other group work.

In addition to this provision of revolving fund, the group organizer is entitled to get Rs. 200/- for one year only to meet her traveling expenses. This amount was however shared equally by the Government of India and the State Government till 1994-95. Out of 3118 groups existing throughout the State, 2335 groups have been provided with revolving fund- in percentage term this is approximately 75 percent. Without the revolving fund a group of poor women cannot undertake any economic activities. Sometimes it is also experienced that for earlier release of revolving fund the groups became defunct as the women members distributed the money within themselves without undertaking any economic activities for additional income generation in favour of their families. Before the group becomes stable and a strong sense of bondage with the members is built up, any release of revolving fund (even in phases) may hamper the interests of DWCRA programme. Here comes the role of Assistant Project Officer (Women Development) at DRDA level, Gram Sevikas at the block level and women panchayat members at the village level to extend their support so that the groups may take concrete shape.

District position of revolving fund (RF) release vis-à-vis total number of groups are presented in Table 5 wherefrom it can be seen that performance of districts in releasing RF varies from one to the other. This variation is sure to effect the group performance also. Along with the release of RF, use of this fund by the groups is also very important. This information is also presented side by side. When the utilization of RF and the number of groups existing are studied, a picture about the working of DWCRA programme will emerge.

This closely approximates the field situations. See Table below.

Table 5

Release and Utilisation of Revolving Fund by DWCRA Groups: District-wise (Since in.ception to 1998-99)

District	*Total No. of Groups*	*No. of groups in whose favour RF released*	*No. of groups utilizing RF*	*Percentage of groups utilizing RF vis-a-vis total no. of Groups*
Coach Behar	140	104	63	60.58
Jalpaiguri	914	676	418	61.90
Darjeeling	516	385	254	65.93
Uttar Dinajpur	234	175	127	72.57
Dakshin Dinajpur	644	480	320	66.67
Malda	415	310	202	65.16
Murshidabad	279	208	136	65.38
Nadia	225	143	118	82.76
North 24 Pargnas	741	581	445	76.59
South 24 Pargnas	503	373	285	76.40
Howrah	1291	1183	975	82.42

Hooghly	455	387	298	77.00
Midnapur	537	404	311	76.98
Bankura	870	646	536	82.97
Purulia	1163	869	667	76.75
Burdwan	320	241	198	82.15
Birbhum	423	318	212	66.67
Total	9670	7483	5565	77.83

Source: Panchayats and Rural Development Dept. Govt. of West Bengal, 1999.

From the Table it can be seen that on an average at the State level slightly above 77 percent of the groups are assisted by revolving fund. In Bankura and Purulia districts, where the programme was launched first, groups assisted with RF were around 75 percent. At the end of the year 1998-99 there remained a gap of 2187 between the groups formed and the groups who received RF. This is mainly due to the fact that the RF is not released in time and a group has to wait for more than one year to get any financial assistance from the Government. Even after getting assistance the groups receiving the assistance are not utilizing the amount for their benefits. The field experience is that after getting the money they kept it in their saving passbooks in Banks and do not even hold meeting to finalise the activities to be taken up. At the state level, on an average only about 48 percent groups are actually utilizing the RF for the purpose of the economic benefits of the group members. In Nadia district the utilization is the highest followed by Purulia district. In Bankura district where the programme was launched in the year 1983-84 along with Purulia, only 23.19 percent of total groups are actually utilizing the fund for the purpose. Thus the use of revolving fund by the groups is not so encouraging and the same varies widely from one district to another. Efficient use of RF is must for making economic activities of DRCRA programme useful. Timely release of funds by DRDA is also equally important for the success of the programme as a group without any income generating activities will soon loose its vibrancy and turns into a dormant group. It is also experienced at the ground level that even if the funds are given, the group simply distributes the fund within the group members as small loans without any arrangements for group monitoring and follow-up and even control over the pattern of utilization of the resources. The grass root reality is that after providing the RF, nobody starting from the panchayat at the village level, block functionaries at the block level and DRDA officials at the district level is interested to take care of the groups of poor women.

Economics Activities

Participation of women in economic activities is a means towards their empowerment. In DWCRA also enough scope exists within the programme for their participation in economic activities. If their participation in economic activity is assured their income will automatically be augmented. Hence the women must be recognized as the workers and not as household workers only. For this in DWCRA thrust is being given on economic activities of women. But the selection of the right activity is very crucial for the individual members of the groups, and the group itself. The field experiences have shown that in certain DWCRA groups, where women are involved in activities and where market support and financial linkages have been ensured adequately, the success is very much ensured. In West Bengal till the end of the year 1993-94 slightly more than 50 percent groups were engaged in some types of income generating activities. During this period 89.24 percent of the groups were engaged in one or some kind of economic activities. Bankura and Purulia, though being the first two districts where the programme was launched, in respect of coverage of members with economic activities they lag behind Jalpaiguri district where DWCRA was started in the year 1986-87. In South 24 Parganas where DWCRA was launched even after Jalpaiguri it has become possible to link up 84.69 percent of groups with economic activities. Collective action alone by the women members may not ensure success of the programme. The pooling of efforts of various agencies working in the same area with the same objectives, i.e., development of the area and the women of that area, improves the chances of success. Linkages and convergence of other developmental and employment generation schemes like IRDP and TRYSEM (for self employment) and JRY (for wage employment) with DWCRA will ensure better success of the programme. In spite of repeated thrusts, the implementation of DWCRA does not give full recognition of the need for convergence with other programmes. The main reason for such lack of dovetailing is that the programmes implementing agencies fail to realize that without converging different programmes and integrating their benefits it would not be possible to bring lasting solution to the problems. For example, even if DWCRA is a sub - scheme of IRDP, there was little integration between the two programmes though Rural Development Department both at the center and the state. DRDA and block set - ups are entrusted with implementation of the programme. Sometimes it is also felt that the panchayat functionaries are very much reluctant to sponsor DWCRA members for IRDP benefits. Most of them believe that once a woman was brought under DWCRA she will be getting assistance under the programme, so her inclusion under IRDP means second assistance. The Panchayat members mostly do not prefer to converge the programme assistance on a person, as they believe in benefiting more number of persons, rather to say consolidating the benefits of the different programmes through convergence. This is the greatest weakness of the rural development programmes in West Bengal as in West Bengal the Panchayat bodies have been given the responsibilities to identify beneficiaries of the programme. Again, women members also in many cases are afraid of undertaking income generating activities for several reasons, which may be categorised as follows.

(a) They do not want to be indebted by getting bank loans;
(b) They think that their products will not have enough price as their designs are inferior and in the competition these products will have low value;

(c) They do not have enough skill and equipments which may debar them from making their products competitive and attractive;

(d) They cannot arrange for enough raw materials whenever it is required because its collection is time consuming.

(e) There is none to look after their children if they have to devote more time to collection of raw materials and marketing of finished products.

All these reasons are closely inter-connected and have their influence on each other. The women alone cannot come out of this vicious circle and for obvious reasons they prefer not to undertake any income generating activities and remain satisfied where they are. Here is the need for intervention from the Government sector and it is expected that functionaries with the responsibilities for implementing the scheme should anticipate these fears of the women and help them to build up the confidence among themselves who have so far remained incapacitated. It is very sad to point out that the functionaries of rural development most often fail to rise to the expectations. No doubt that the marketing of products is one of the most critical areas in DWCRA for implementing the economic activities component of the programme. It may be that Govt. itself cannot bear the whole responsibility of the work, but certainly the Govt. agencies can build up a support network, which in turn will absorb the products of DWCRA and may be the assured sources of marketing for the poor, inarticulate women. In this network building DRDAs should function as the coordinator because of their pivotal role in rural development at the district level. To name a few such promotional agencies are State Small Scale Industries Corporation, Khadi and Village Industries Commission at the central level and Khadi and Village Industries Board at the state level, Weavers Cooperative Societies, Handicrafts Board, Coir Board etc. Arrangements for periodic review of the situation and quick response on the point of difficulties by DRDAs may prove to be a step in the right direction. For upgradation of the quality of products DRDAs should arrange for skill training of women members, (but sufficient caution must be exercised so that DWCRA does not mean skill training only). This convergence does not occur timely and adequately. In West Bengal varied economic activities (at present 89 types) are being undertaken by women groups, some are traditional in nature and some are innovative also (list of such activities is given in annexure I). The traditional activities usually do not pay much because of traditional and low level skills and wide spread availability of the products. This indicates that proper selection of activity is very much crucial to the success of the programmes, and for making the selection, the back-up support should come from the Panchayat women members at the village level, Gram Sevika and Lady Extension Officer at the block level and specially Assistant Project Officer (Women Development) of DRDA at the district level. However, the experience is that the help of the trio is not readily available for this purpose in initiating and sustaining the economic activities of the groups. The feeling of loneliness thus persists within the women even after their coverage in DWCRA. It seems that the programme itself tends to be victim of gender discrimination as the heads of the offices of most of the agencies are male and they most often attach less priority to this programme exclusively designed for betterment of the rural poor women.

Administrative Infrastructure

For administering the programme at the block level there are Gram Sevikas and to supervise the work of Gram Sevikas, there are Mukhya Sevikas now known as Lady Extension Officer, Social Education (LEOSE). But the Gram Sevika is the key person in the implementation of the programme at the grass-root level. In the manual for the Gram Sevika in DWCRA (1991) published by the Govt. of India, certain roles of Gram Sevikas are prescribed in relation to the group members of the DWCRA.

They are as follows:

The Gram Sevikas should:

— help poor women to be vocal and get them united for discussion and action.

— help to develop self-confidence within group members, as self-confidence will lead to self-reliance in actions of women.

— help women group members to analyse their situations and objectives and strategies on which the women have to work for their upliftment.

In most of the blocks of the state, the Gram Sevikas became less effective for one reason or other. The most important factor that influences the effectiveness of the working of Gram Sevikas is that in majority of the blocks, the Gram Sevikas have come very near the superannuation and the State Govt. have also not recruited Gram Sevikas for a long time. As a result the actual number of Gram Sevikas vis-à-vis the sanctioned strength is getting reduced in a regular manner. This affects the programme implementation very much. On the one hand for achieving the target of group formation set by the Govt. the block agencies are forming the groups and on the other hand due to dwindling number of Gram Sevikas effective support cannot be extended to the groups formed. The result is the less qualitative implementation of the programme. The situation is also very much discomfortable in respect of the strength of LEOSE as out of twelve districts (at the end of 1993-94) implementing DWCRA, in 7 districts the available strength of LEOSE is less than half of the sanctioned strength. At the village level, in fact there is none to provide support to the poor women brought under the programme. Through the Panchayat election in 1993, large numbers of women were brought to the fold of Panchayats (one third reservation for women was made for all the three tiers of the Panchayat institutions at village, block and district level). But they are also very new to the system and till now nothing significant has happened due to their interventions.

At the district level there is one Assistant Project Officer (Women Development) in DRDA. Because of the organizational structure designed in a way to include women only, APO (WD) obviously should be a woman. APO (WD) must be a prime mover of DWCRA, rather to say, DWCRA in the district would flourish with her best efforts and imaginations. According to the Manual for APO in DWCRA, the roles of an APO have been perceived as follows:

As a Motivator

This covers both the field level workers, e.g., LEOSE and Gram Sevikas at block levels and the DWCRA groups in the village.

As a Planner and Manager

APO (WD) should ensure timely flows of various inputs to the groups for the successful implementation of the programme. Apart from overall supervision, the APO (WD) should build up a reporting system for constant monitoring and evaluation of the programme down to the village level.

As a Coordinator

For the success of the programme, support from different development agencies are a must and APO has to co-ordinate all these agencies so that their supports may converge on women groups for sustainable benefit.

As a Facilitator

This role is performed mainly with the help of functionaries under her and other support agencies working for the proper implementation of the programme—to name a few such agencies are banking institutions, voluntary Organisations, Panchayati Raj bodies etc.

As a Source of Information

Lack of access to information is a formidable disadvantage to women. When the women groups require information on different topics concerning their status and upliftment, APO (WD), through her agency, has to meet the demand of the women groups.

As an Awareness Builder

APO (WD), it is expected, should emerge as an important source of awareness building of rural women who themselves are not completely aware of their situations and positions. APO (WD) should harness the services of LEOSE, Gram Sevikas, Women Panchayat Members and Group Organisers of DWCRA to the fullest possible extent.

For achieving this goal adequate arrangements for training of functionaries (both officials and non-officials) along with group organizers and a second member from each group have to be made, and APO (WD) has the responsibility to plan and implement these training programmes. Therefore, an APO (WD) has to perform multiple roles of an educator, friend, philosopher and guide of DWCRA groups and the members of the groups. In the real field, however APO (WD) is bogged down with various other work of DRDA, which sometimes has very little relevance to the DWCRA. Even in some DRDAs, the post of APO (WD) is not filled up and one APO of DRDA has to fill - up the gap on temporary basis as a result of which the programme interests are only jeopardized.

Training: An Essential Input

For proper orientation of the functionaries and the group organizers elaborate training is of urgent need. Keeping this in view, the training programmes in West Bengal have been thoroughly revamped. The services of non-governmental organizations are also being drafted into the training programmes so far dominated by government officials. The process of change in training structure was initiated after a detailed examination of the existing concept, content and method of training. From the traditional system of training in the Govt. system where training is synonymously treated with teaching (trainer is nothing but an instructor), training in DWCRA is being made participatory training which is nothing but an extension of participatory philosophy of development to training. The introduction of participatory training in DWCRA makes the participants (whether they are Gram Sevikas and LEOSE, or Women Panchayat Members, Pradhans, or group leaders and any members of the group or APO looking after the women development) faithful to the philosophy of participation, helps them to realize the necessity of participation and so on and so forth. For ensuring singularity of the participation level (at least at the district level) all Assistant Project Officers (WD) have been brought under the district level trainers' team. As APO (WD) has a wide range of experience about the working of the programme throughout the district, her inclusion in the training team will become an important source of knowledge for the other participants in the district level training. In DWCRA, NGOs are also integrated with the process of training because they have considerable experience of working with the poor and organising them for forging ahead. The Seventh Five-Year Plan expressly recognized this. But in West Bengal, in the case of DWCRA it began to take shape only from the later part of the year 1993 (the second year of the Eighth Five-Year Plan). Most of the districts implementing DWCRA have identified one suitable NGO for accommodating it as facilitator in the training programme. Two or three trainers from NGOs along with APO (WD) of the district form the training team. Thus it has become possible to establish an effective linkage between GO and NGOs. District-wise list of NGOs organizing training is given below:

	District	*Name of NGOs*
1.	North 24 Parganas	Gram Seva Sangha, Hatthuba
2.	South 24 Parganas	Sunderban Khadi and Village Industries Society, Canning
3.	Birbhum	Elmhirst Institute of Community Studies, Shantiniketan
4.	Bankura	Gandhi Vichar Parishad

5.	Murshidabad	Development Dialogue
6.	Midnapur	Seva Bharati Krishi Vigyan Kendra, Midnapore, Haldi Samaj Kalyan Parishad,Durga Chak
7.	Nadia	Sree Ma Mahila Samiti, Duttapulia

Source: Information collected from respective DRDAs of the concerned Districts

In Jalpaiguri, Burdwan and Hooghly the government institutions are organising the training programme. As there is no reputed NGO in Purlia district for taking responsility of such training, NGOs of Bankura are bearing this responsibility. Integration of NGO in the training programme partially serves the objective of involvement of voluntary organizations with the programme for women development. Associating NGOs with the programme planning and implementation can only ensure full NGO involvement with the programme. Partial involvement sometimes hampers the smooth progress of the program as there lies the scope for emergence of differences in opinion between GO and NGO. Training alone is not the panacea of all ills of the programme. Rather training needs the support of other components of the programme structure viz. strong motivation on the part of the Govt. functionaries to work for the poor rural women, determination of the administering agencies to extend support to rural women in their efforts for changing their prevailing situations etc.

Conclusion and Suggestions

From the above study it can be well understood that the programme of DWCRA is yet to achieve its success as it is expected. Though the groups have to be formed for fulfilling the targets set from above, qualitatively these groups are not that much sound to accomplish the objectives of the programme, i.e., emancipation of women and thereby elevation in their status. The main reason for such state of affairs is the lack of true understanding about the programme and the proneness to interpret the programme in the individual's way.

For improving the quality of implementation of the programme everyone concerned with the programme needs to have a common understanding of the objectives of the programme, and this can be achieved through intensified training of all categories starting from the group organisers and members to the Block Development Officers, Savapatis of Panchayat Samities, Project Officer and Assistant Project Officers of DRDA. It is desirable that the project implementating agencies should first empower themselves with the clear understanding of the objectives of the programme and then make efforts to inculcate this into the minds of the programme beneficiaries. The gap in understanding needs to be bridged forthwith as already more than twelve years have gone.

In the overall set-up of development administration, DWCRA programme is receiving low priority. This is nothing exceptional from the normal situation. As in patriarchal society males dominate every field including administration, so any programme exclusively for development of women would receive low priority. But attitudinal change must come and this programme should get at least that priority which other rural development programmes are getting. This programme must be reviewed not as a programme launched as a token of sympathy for the rural poor women but as a programme in the greater interest of the society. It must be appreciated that the problems faced by women are not solely the problems of women—they are the problems of society as a whole. The stark reality is that the official functionaries most often fail to internalize the deprivation of women and accept the programme just like other routine work. Involvement of NGOs can help to improve the situation as they have better understanding of the existing situations, close intimacy with the people in common and greater dedication for the cause of the people than the government functionaries. It should be believed that the poor women have enough potentialities; only requirement is that the rural development agencies should provide them with the continuous support and services so that they may turn into strong vibrant groups.

Linkages of DWCRA with other programmes are also essential because DWCRA itself is a programme designed for making convergence with other programmes in the sense that the groups must be developed in such a way that they can become an effective and conscious receiving system for channelising and dovetailing benefits of all programmes meant for the poor rural women. Though this convergence is very much desired but in the field level it occurs very rarely. For example, though the name of the programme itself includes development of children, but in reality it has become a programme for development of women alone. It is desirable that along with women, children also need adequate attention (this emphasis makes possible integration of ICDS and DWCRA).

In our country, since inception of the planning era, many programmes were initiated for the development of the poor. But the tragedy is that poor are not aware of the benefits offered by the Govt. This awareness-building component is never taken care of adequately; different functional departments do not even give recognition to it properly. This is true of DWCRA programme also. Therefore, awareness building among the women groups is not only the priority of the programme and its objectives but above all the situation of the women should get appropriate attention of the functionaries. This work may be entrusted to voluntary organisations as they have rich experience in these fields.

For making DWCRA programme an effective tool for amelioration of miseries of rural women all - out ventures should be made by the government along with the people and the non-government agencies. Philosophically this is an ideal programme for women development. However, recently since April 1999 the programme has changed and a new programme in the name of SGSY has been introduced. Under this programme Self - help Groups (SHGs) have been formed to carry out different activities. Most of the states have converted their earlier DWCRA group into SHGs, which was permitted during the first year of the new programme as per guideline. The programme is yet to complete its three years; hence, we are unable to comment about the progress. The programme for women development is well designed, but in practice it is very difficult to implement it appropriately as a lot of dynamics are involved in the formation of groups and its subsequent development. For its better implementation the programme requires constant care and support from all associated with rural development.

NOTES

The coverage of the programme (DWCRA) by the end of September 1994 was 442 districts spread all over the country. Later on it covered in all the districts by the end of VII Plan.

REFERENCES

Prasad, C.H. (et.al) *Development of Women and Children in Rural Areas*, New Delhi; Discovery Publishing House, 1996; pp. 1-2

Reddy, S. & C. Renuka, DWCRA-A Book for Rural Women, Yojana, Dec. 5, 1994.

ANNEXURE –I

	Name of the activities	*District*
1.	Wooden spoon making	Malda
2.	Yarn from waste cocoon	Malda
3.	Khadi weaving	Darjeeling
4.	Floriculture	Darjeeling
5.	Jari work	Hooghly
6.	Chickon embroidery	Hooghly
7.	Fish hook making	Purulia
8.	Sericulture	Purulia
9.	Dhokra Craft	Jalpaiguri

contd...

contd...

	Name of the activities	*District*
10.	Detergent making	North 24 Parganas
11.	Refill making	North 24 Paraganas
12.	Macranne	Birbhum, Bhurdwan
13.	Wooden handicrafts	Birbhum
14.	Feather Crafts	South 24 Parganas
15.	Plastic Fancy Flower making	South 24 Parganas

Source: Data Collected from DRDA Office of the respective Districts.

V

Women Empowerment through Literacy

Literacy is power and illiteracy is disability. According to 1991 census directives "a person who can both read and write with understanding in any language is to be taken as literate. A person who can merely read but cannot write is not literate". Again mere ability to sign one's name is not adequate to qualify a person as being able to write with understanding. These definitions of literacy are followed in the context of the present study. Similarly, on the basis of 1991 census guidelines a person is illiterate if he or she can neither read nor write, or can merely read but cannot write in any language. Education holds the key to an improvement in position in society and is accepted as a passport to a better life. Therefore, it is strongly desired for any betterment of the society as a whole; ignorance and poverty go hand in hand: a person is poor because he is ignorant and he is ignorant because he is poor. Only Literacy has the power to break this vicious circle. According to Frank Lauback, an American missionary "literacy is a tool to be used in everyday life; a tool to be constantly sharpened and perfected so that it becomes a person's constant companion". Thus, literacy is more than an end in itself. It is the foundation for human development and life-long march towards systematic betterment of the individuals, of the societies and of the country as whole. Obviously, the most urgent priority is to ensure access to and improve the quality of learning, particularly the education of girls and women community so that obstacles in the way of empowerment of weaker sections may be removed at any cost. Among the poorest, literacy has important ramifications in better employment opportunities, higher productivity in agricultural activities, better health status through reduction in child mortality rate, participatory role of women and enhanced the overall standard of living.

Objectives of the Study

With this background the present study has been taken up in Birbhum district of West Bengal. The study is mainly concentrated on Intergrated Rural Development Programme, a major strategy for poverty alleviation in rural India.

The study aims at the following:

(a) To reflect how literate persons appropriate more benefits of the programme;
(b) To assess the awareness level of IRDP schemes holder families;
(c) To examine asset utilization pattern of the programme beneficiaries and its relationship with literacy;
(d) To feel the impact of income generation and asset formation of IRDP beneficiaries: and
(e) To have a look on the access of IRDP beneficiaries towards skill development vis-à-vis their literacy status.

Methodology

For the purpose of the study six blocks of the district were chosen on the basis of their performance in IRDP during the year 1989-90. From three sub-divisions (Suri, Bolpur and Rampurhat) of the district one better performing block and one relatively poorly performing block were selected to wipe out any biasness in block selection. From each block 40 beneficiaries out of the total beneficiaries assisted during the Year 1989-90 were considered as representative samples. Hence, sample size becomes 240. Of 240 beneficiaries for male–female study

40 per cent i.e., 96 are female beneficiaries and the rest 144 are males. During seventh Plan period stipulation is that 40 per cent of total families assisted should be women beneficiaries. Hence, in this study this reservation is followed. At the time of selection of schemes all the sectoral activities (Primary, Secondary and Tertiary) are accepted.

Literacy Scenario of the Study District

Since independence, this district holds a very low literacy rate profile with 1.4 per cent only as mentioned in the first census of 1951. In 1961, this literacy rate went up to 22.09 per cent. It is indicated in this census that in the rural areas of the district there were 206 persons per 1000 were literate for every total population as against 167 persons per 1000 of total population in 1951. As observed by 1961 District Census Handbook that education is, as might be expected, far more widely disseminated amongst the urban than rural population (Dutta and Ghosh: 1995:33-43).

In 1971 census the literacy rate of the district rose to 26.57 per cent. This indicates a decadal growth of 20.28 per cent. In 1981 census the literacy rate of the district was 33.69 per cent, that is, a growth of 26.80 per cent during the period 1971-1981. In 1991 census the literacy rate in the district further rose to 39.31 per cent i.e. a decadal variation of 16.68 per cent.

In contrast the female literacy rate was only 6.80 per cent, which further rose to 29.98 per cent in 1991. But during 1961 to 1981, the rates were respectively 11.47 per cent, 17.40 per cent and 24.46 per cent only. Of course, in each of the decades there was some progress, but it is not that remarkable. This low rate can also be corroborated by sex ratio of literacy i.e. number of literate females per 1000 male literates. In 1951 ratio of literacy was 231. In 1961 the number increased to 344, in 1971 census it rose to 475, in 1981, it was 552 and finally in 1991 census it reached 589. If female literacy in respect of scheduled caste community be taken into account, it was 1.89 percent in 1961, 4.57 per cent in 1971 and 7.42 per cent in 1981. In case of scheduled tribe community literacy rates for females were 0.50 per cent in 1961, 0.93 per cent in 1971 and 2.25 per cent in 1981. Thus, powerlessness of women can easily be apprehended. Even within women community there is biasness in favour of urban women. In 1991 census while the female literacy rate in rural areas is 28.11 per cent, the corresponding rate in urban areas is 49.10 per cent i.e. a gap of 1.75 times. In 1951, urban female literacy was three times more than rural female literacy (6.40 per cent in rural and 18.52 per cent in urban areas). This trend was more or less continued in 1961 census also (10.18 per cent in rural, 30.12 per cent in urban). In 1971, the gap was slightly reduced, as the rate of urban female literacy was 2.45 times that of rural female literacy (15.85 per cent in rural and 38.92 per cent in urban areas). In 1981 it was further reduced, as rural female literacy rate was 22.94 per cent in comparison to urban female literacy rate of 41.70 per cent.

Male-female anomaly in literacy rates is depicted in the statement below. This indicates preponderance of literate males in the society, which signifies greater control of affairs of the society by males.

Year	*Male literacy rate (in percentage)*	*Female literacy rate (in percentage)*
1951	28.22	6.80
1961	32.43	11.47
1971	35.45	17.40
1981	42.58	24.46
1991	48.15	29.98

With the above backdrop let us now go into the study results.

Analysis

i. Literacy Status of beneficiaries

In Table 1 literacy status of the sample families is given vis-à-vis male and female beneficiaries. From the Table below

Table : 1
Literacy Status of Families

Sl.No	*Block*	*Illiterate*		*Literate*		*Total*	
		Male	*Female*	*Male*	*Female*	*Male*	*Female*
1.	Suri-II	13	11	11	5	24	16
2.	Dubrajpur	15	10	9	6	24	16
3.	Bolpur-Sriniketan	14	9	10	7	24	16
4.	Labpur	11	12	13	4	24	16
5.	Rampurhat-II	10	11	14	5	24	16
6.	Mayureswar-II	12	13	12	3	24	16
	Total	75	66	69	30	144	96

it can be seen that of 144 males, 75 are illiterate: in percentage term illiteracy rate within male beneficiaries is 52.08 while illiteracy rate within female beneficiaries is 68.75 per cent. Picture of formal education within literates' beneficiaries is presented in Table 2. All the literates have some formal education and that too is biased heavily in favour of men as out 69 literate men 24 i.e. 34.78 per cent have education up to secondary and above. In the case of female literates only 3 i.e. 10 per cent achieved this standard. Formal educational qualifications are strongly desired for attaining improved status in the society. Most of the women literate beneficiaries, (73.33 per cent), have schooling up to primary standard. This is precisely because of the fact that in rural areas more importance is attached to education of boys than girls; in other words there are wide scale gender disparities. In the case of poor families this is more pertinent (see Table–2).

Though education is a major force in redefining women's role and status, yet women are deprived more in receiving formal education due to less prioritisation of their needs in poor families. Besides economic factors it is felt that social and cultural rigidities are responsible for such inequalities. Availabil-

Table 2

Education Standard of Beneficiaries

Sl. No	*Block*	*Upto Primary*		*Upto Class-Viii*		*Upto Secondary*		*Upto Higher Secondary*		*Upto Graduate*		*Above Graduate*		*Total*	
		Male	*Female*	*Male*	*Female*	*Male*	*Female*	*Male*	*Female*	*Male*	*Female*	*Male*	*Female*	*Male*	*Female*
1.	Suri-II	2	4	3	1	2	X	3	X	1	X	X	X	11	5
2.	Dubrajpur	4	5	2	1	2	X	1	X	X	X	X	X	9	6
3.	Bolpur-Sriniketan	4	3	3	2	1	2	2	X	X	X	X	X	10	7
4.	Labpur	5	4	4	X	2	X	2	X	X	X	X	X	13	4
5.	Rampurhat-II	4	3	5	1	3	1	2	X	X	X	X	X	14	5
6.	Mayureswar-II	5	3	4	X	3	X	X	X	X	X	X	X	12	3
	Total	24	22	21	5	13	3	10	X	1	X	X	X	69	30

M=Male F= Female

ity of equal educational opportunities only can lead to women's assumption of a range of social roles. In this present study only one male beneficiary becomes able to reach graduation standard as against no women. Differentials in education reflect gender inequity throughout the system.

ii. Quantum of investment and Pre-assistance income

In Table 3 beneficiaries are distributed on the basis of their pre-assistance income vis-à-vis literacy status. From the Table it can be seen that of 69 literate males 3 belonging to above cut off line income were able to garner benefits of IRDP. This is a case of irregularity. 56 per cent of illiterate males belong to the lowest category income while in the case of literate males 57.97 per cent belong to income range of Rs. 2266 to 3500 and Rs. 3501 to 4800. This implies that literate persons of higher income range received assistance under IRDP. The relevant percentage figure in the case of literate males is 44 only. Literacy thus helps affluent section within the poor to get programme assistance. This is quite in contradiction to the programme norm of assistance by which the families in the lowest strata of income should be assisted first. It is presumed that literate people have better access to Panchayats who are authorised to select beneficiaries. Illiterate people by character are mostly shy and introvert.

Table 3
Distribution of Beneficiaries over Pre-investment Income vis-a-vis Literacy Status

Range of Per Annum Income (in Rs.)	*Illiterate*		*Literate*		*Total*	
	Male	*Female*	*Male*	*Female*	*Male*	*Female*
0-2265	42	39	28	18	68	57
2265-3500	25	27	27	9	52	36
3501-4800	8	X	13	3	21	3
Above 4800	X	X	3	X	3	X
Total	75	66	69	30	144	96

In the case of female beneficiaries also something happened. Most of the female illiterate (59.09 per cent) have pre-investment income in the range 0-2265 (destitute group). Even with literacy, women have less power than men as more than 50 percent of women belong to the lowest rung of the income range. However, 5 literate women (16.8 %) out of the total female literate beneficiaries of higher income range become able to get them selected for assistance under IRDP. The Table thus, reflects literacy biasness at the time of selection. See Table-3.

Not only literate people of higher income range become able to be identified for assistance, but also they appropriated more of investment in the programme. Higher value schemes are normally endowed to literate beneficiaries. In Table 4 information on quantum of assistance is given.

Table 4
Distribution of Beneficiaries on the Basis of Quantum of investment.

Range of Per Investment (in Rupees)	*Illiterate*		*Literate*		*Total*	
	Male	*Female*	*Male*	*Female*	*Male*	*Female*
Upto 3000	7	11	4	6	11	17
3001-4000	9	14	9	6	18	20
4001-5000	33	31	11	12	44	43
5001-6000	18	10	15	4	33	14
6001-7000	5	X	8	2	1	3 2
7001-8000	3	X	13	X	16	X
8001-9000	X	X	7	X	7	X
Above 9000	X	X	2	X	2	X
Total	75	66	69	30	144	96

In the case of 2 literate males, investment (subsidy plus bank loan) under the programme is more than Rs. 9000. Out of 69 literate males the investment of 45 (65.22 per cent) was more than Rs. 5000 per beneficiary. In the case of literate females 84.85 per cent received assistance (subsidy and loan taken together) upto the maximum of Rs. 5000. This implies that women were provided with traditional and low value schemes like rice processing (Kutial), muri making etc. If per beneficiary investment be calculated then it can be seen that in the case of illiterate males it is Rs. 4593/- only. While in the case of literate male it is Rs. 5748/-, the gain of literate males is thus 25.10 per cent. In the case of lititerate female beneficiaries, per beneficiary investment is Rs. 3939/- while that in the case of literate female is Rs. 3976/-. Gain of literate female is thus 0.71 per cent. This signifies that in the case of male beneficiaries literacy is a strong factor to grab more assistance while in the case of female literacy it is not so strong a factor to get more investment.

There are many other reasons namely, social and cultural, which inhibits rural women to speak for themselves. Relative status of women is very much cocooned in our tradition bound social system. In the case of male beneficiaries per beneficiary investment in the programme is Rs. 5145/- while per female beneficiaries investment is only Rs. 3947/-. Thus male bias in the programme can be noticed. Another fact, which comes out from the Table, is that in the case of literates beneficiary investment is more here; per literate beneficiary investment is Rs. 5207/- while investment per illiterate beneficiary is Rs. 4287/-. Thus literacy is a key factor at the time of investment in the programme.

iii. Awareness of Beneficiaries

If the mode of selection of scheme (Table 5) is considered, illiterate beneficiaries have no options in respect of schemes selected for them; due to lack of knowledge they have no preference at all. Whatever be given to them, they are satisfied with it. In the case of illiterate beneficiaries 78.72 per cent schemes are finalised by Panchayat body members; whereas in the case of literate beneficiaries Panchyat bodies finalise 67.71 per cent schemes. Male-Female break-up is also given to reflect dependency of women. In the case of illiterate females outsiders finalise 95.45 per cent schemes (Panchayat, Bank, Block Officials) while in the case of literate females, 86.67 per cent of schemes are finalised by these agencies.

Table 5
Mode of Selection of Schemes: Responses of Beneficiaries.

Mode of Selection	*Illiterate*		*Literate*		*Total*	
	Male	*Female*	*Male*	*Female*	*Male*	*Female*
On the basis of Beneficiaries Options	X	X	15	2	15	2
Finalised by Panchayats	58	53	41	24	99	77
Finalised by Banks	8	9	4	2	12	11
Suggested by Block Officials	2	1	1	X	3	1
Finalised by Relations/ Friend of Beneficiaries	7	3	8	2	15	5
Total	75	66	69	30	144	96

With the help of marking technique (1 mark for response Yes and O for No) in this study awareness level of male and female beneficiaries has been measured. Total marks in the case of male are 720 (5x144) and in the case of female are 480 (5x96). Counting Yes responses marks gained by male beneficiaries become 296 while in the case of female beneficiaries it becomes 122; thus percentage of marks secured by males is 41.11 and by female 25.42. Such is the state of affairs in respect of awareness level of beneficiaries. Here literate-illiterate break-up is not given, as among illiterate beneficiaries practically there exists no awareness about the programme objectives and programme provisions. Responses of beneficiaries towards their awareness are given in Table 6 below:

Table 6
Awareness Level of IRDP Beneficiaries: Responses to Questions

Item	Male		Female		Total	
	Yes	*No*	*Yes*	*No*	*Yes*	*No*
1. Do you know that beneficiaries are to be selected on the basis of the poorest to the poor norm?	66	78	27	69	93	147
2. Do you know provisions of 102 IRDP subsidy admissibility?	102	42	41	55	143	97
3. Do you know that schemes are to be sanctioned on the basis of beneficiaries' need and choice?	52	92	39	57	91	149
4. Do you hear about TRYSEM Scheme?	71	73	15	81	86	154
5. Do you know that there is provision of consumption loan in IRDP?	5	139	X	96	5	235
Total	296	424	122	357	428	782

Communication is the foundation of all organised actions. But in the case of illiterate persons access to communication is very meager. In the case of illiterate males 38.66 per cent have access to communication while only 4.54 per cent illiterate females have access to communication network and 50 per cent female literates have, such access. If male-female aspects were taken into account, then 50.68 per cent males have access to different communication systems while only 18.75 per cent females have such access. Thus, women have a very marginal role in the process of communication; literates rely more on audio-visual media. Responses of beneficiaries in respect of access to communication network are given in table 7.

Table 7
Access to Communication Network: Distribution of Sample Families

Communication Media	*Illiterate*		*Literate*		*Total*	
	Male	*Female*	*Male*	*Female*	*Male*	*Female*
Newspaper	5	X	18	3	23	3
Radio	15	3	15	9	30	12
Television	9	X	6	3	15	3
Magazines	X	X	5	X	5	X
Total	29	3	44	15	73	18

iv. Asset utilization Pattern and impact of Literacy

Literacy and utilisation pattern of assets endowed under the programme through bank loan and government subsidy have positive correlation. This is amply reflected in Table 8. 58 per cent of male literates and 70 per cent of female literates have assets at the time of field observation during the study (field visit was made in the early months of the current year). Utilisation of assets to a larger extent is due to impact of literacy. A literate person can preconceive things well and have the power to assess his needs and objectives of the programme. In the case of illiterate persons, schemes were mostly thrusted upon. In those cases the ground is not ready yet. Non-existent automatically is very high. In the case of male literates the rate of non-existence is 22.67 per cent as against 30.44 per cent in the case of illiterates. Again in the case of female literates the rate of non-existence is 13.33 whereas in the case of female illiterates it is more than double (28.78 per cent). If male–female dichotomy is considered then it can be visualised that females are better users of programmes than their male counterparts. The rate of existence of assets is higher in the case of female beneficiaries than the males. See Table 8 below:

Table 8
Asset Utilization Pattern in IRDP.

Status of Assets	*Illiterate*		*Literate*		*Total*	
	Male	*Female*	*Male*	*Female*	*Male*	*Female*
Exist	42	21	35	36	77	57
Not Exist	17	4	21	19	3	8 23
Partially Exist	16	5	13	11	29	16
Total	75	30	69	66	144	96

v. Asset Formation and income Generation

Responses of beneficiaries on asset formation with the help of IRD Programme assistance are given in Table 9 below. Beneficiaries are classified into four categories viz. male literates, female literates, male illiterates and female illiterates.

Table 9
Responses of Beneficiaries on Asset Formation.

Status of Beneficiaries	*Better Housing*		*Purchase of Consumer Durables*		*Land Purchase*	
	Yes	*No*	*Yes*	*No*	*Yes*	*No*
Male Literates	15	54	26	43	7	62
Female Literates	8	22	7	23	X	30
Male Illiterates	3	72	9	66	2	73
Female Illiterates	1	65	X	66	X	66
Total	27	213	42	198	9	231

Asset formation aspect was viewed through three items—better housing facilities after assistance, purchases of consumer durables and purchase of land for cultivation. In the case of male literates 15 (21.74%) responded positively for better housing i.e., it becomes possible to augment housing facilities through extension of new rooms or building a new shelter. In the case of purchase of consumer durables and land purchase, positive responses are available from 37.68% and 10.14% male literates respectively. In the case of female literates, 8 (26.67%) are enjoying better housing but 23.33 per cent became able to purchase new consumer durables for their families. This percentage is less than male literates probably due to little freedom that women enjoy in the matter of decision-making in families. Cases of asset formation in illiterate families are very insignificant, over the sample size. Impact of the programme for better housing is 11.25 per cent, purchase of consumer durables is 12.50 per cent and land purchase is 3.75 percent. In totality, impact of IRD programmes on asset formation is not that significant. Literates alone enjoy whatever impact in this field occurred because a literate person has more ability to manage a situation than an illiterate.

vi. Income Generation Impact

In Table 10 beneficiaries are arranged on the basis of post-assistance income. Income per annum is categorised in five ranges, viz. Rs. 0 - 4000 (destitutes), Rs. 4001-6000 (very very poor) and Rs. 6001-8500 (very poor) and Rs. 8501-11000 (poor). This is Eight Plan classification of poor families in rural areas; per annum income of Rs. 11000 is the poverty line. From the Table it can be seen that only 5 male beneficiaries become able to cross poverty line. Out of these 5 male beneficiaries 4 are literate and one illiterate. Again, only 14 male beneficiaries of which 9 literates and 5 illiterates are in income range of Rs. 8501-11000. Economic positions of women beneficiaries are still worse. There are no women beneficiaries in the highest income range of below poverty line. 95.45 per cent illiterate females belong to the lowest two income ranges, while 40 per cent of literate females are in these two incomes, and 40 per cent of literate females are in these two ranges. Thus, men are better placed than women even after the introduction of IRDP. This indicates male biasness of the programme also.

Table 10
Distribution of Beneficiaries on the Basis of Post Assistance Annual Income.

Range of Income	*Illiterate*		*Literate*		*Total*	
(In Rupees)	*Male*	*Female*	*Male*	*Female*	*Male*	*Female*
0-4000	15	27	11	8	26	35
4001-6000	22	36	14	4	36	40
6001-8500	32	3	31	18	63	21
8500-1100	5	X	9	X	14	X
Above 11000	1	X	4	X	5	X
Total	75	66	69	30	144	96

vii. Access of IRDP Beneficiaries towards Skill Development

In IRD Programme there is a component for development of skills of beneficiaries through training. The scheme is known as Training of Rural Youth for Self-Employment (TRYSEM). Responses of beneficiaries on availability of this scheme are presented in Table 11. Blockwise presentation is given so as to have a detail look. From the Table it can be seen that out of 69 literate males 22 (31.88%) became able to avail themselves of the training opportunities whereas only 4 (5.33 %) out of 75 illiterate males got such training. In the case of female beneficiaries, 7 (23.33%) out of 30 literates became able to get assistance of training scheme and 4 out of 66 illiterates got training for skill development. TRYSEM scheme also has a very strong bias towards males, as out of 144 male beneficiaries 26 (18.85%) received training whereas of 96 females only 11(11.46) received benefits of training progamme. Again among those who received training for developing skills/acquiring new skills, 84.61 per cent are literate in the case of male beneficiaries and in case of female beneficiaries 63.64 per cent are literate. Thus, training scheme helps those who are literate, rather, it can be said that literacy helps beneficiaries to get the opportunity of training for their economic betterment.

Table 11
Responses of Beneficiaries on Availability of Training in Skill Formation.

Block Name	Illiterate		Literate		Total	
	Male	Female	Male	Female	Male	Female
Suri-II	Y-3 N-8	Y-X N-5	Y-2 N-11	Y-X N-11	Y-5 N-19	Y-X N-16
Dubrapur	Y-4 N-8	Y-X N-6	Y-2 N-13	Y-X N-10	Y-3 N-21	Y-X N-16
Bulpur-Sriniketan	Y-4 N-6	Y-5 N-2	Y-X N-14	Y-3 N-6	Y-4 N-20	Y-8 N-8
Labpur	Y-5 N-8	Y-2 N-2	Y-X N-11	Y-5 N-11	Y-5 N-19	Y-3 N-13
Rampurhat-II	Y-7 N-7	Y-X N-5	Y-X N-10	Y-X N-11	Y-X N-17	Y-X N-16
Mayureswar-II	Y-2 N-10	Y-X N-3	Y-X N-12	Y-X N-13	Y-2 N-22	Y-X N-16
Total	Y-25 N-47	Y-7 N-23	Y-4 N-71	Y-8 N-62	Y-19 N-118	Y-11 N-85

Conclusion

From this study it becomes clear that literacy is indispensable for reaping the benefits of any programme, which is meant to meet the needs of the poor. Until and unless programme beneficiaries feel that programmes are meant for them, nothing significant impact can be felt no matter whatever be the size of investment in the programmes. This is the single most reason why the programmes are not picking up to the extent desired by planners and policy makers. This is the cause and effect of dominance of patron-client relationship between programme implementers and beneficiaries of programme. Prevalence of widespread illiteracy forces the rural people to stay in isolation and be satisfied with whatever be given to them. In fact illiteracy forces them to forget their individualities. Thus, the crying need of the day is to make people, in particular rural people, and especially rural female literate. With this end in view Total Literacy Campaign (TLC) has been started in the country. IRDP is to be linked effectively with TLC with the dictum that "Until you are literate you will not get assistance under the programmes". In Birbhum district TLC has been launched for making the district fully literate.

NOTE

1. For further details see, District Census Handbook of Birbhum Dist, West Bengal, 1961.

REFERENCES

Dutta, S.K. and D. K. Ghosh, 'Status of Women in Total Literacy Campaign: A Study of Birbhum District in West Bengal', Journal of Rural Development, Vol, 14 (i), pp.33-43, 1995.

VI

Women in Panchayat

The concept of Panchayat Raj Institutions is an age-old phenomenon. But the uniqueness of these institutions at present is emergence of large number of village women as members. This has been possible only due to the 73rd Amendment to the Constitution of India brought about in the year 1993. However, in West Bengal the basic philosophy of the 73rd Amendment was well taken into account only in the last Panchayat Election held in the month of May 1993. Before delving into the study it is worth mentioning that West Bengal is the only state in the country where the elections to the three-tier institutions were held consecutively for the fourth time starting from way back in 1978 (just one year after the present Left Front-led Government was voted to power). Though all the provisions of the 73rd Amendment were not followed as election was held prior to its effect, the Government of West Bengal made the provisions for reserving not less than one third seats of Panchayat bodies at each tier, viz. village, block and district level, for women. The objective is to bring hitherto sidelined women community into the mainstream of development efforts (both planning and implementation). Earlier to this election representation of women in Panchayat bodies was very insignificant. In the earlier set-up there was provision for inclusion of two women members as nominated members if there was no women representation. If in a Panchayat body there was only one member, then one woman would be nominated as member. As a consequence of such anomalous representation in the gamut of development efforts women had very little to contribute both in the decision-making and implementation. To remove such discrepancies, the Government of West Bengal made this reservation for bringing rural women into the forum for development of rural areas.

To have an idea about the things prevalent in the periods prior to 1993, representation of women in Panchayat Raj Institutions of Birbhum District vis-à-vis total members are presented below:

Year	*Zilla Parishad*		*Panchayat Samiti*		*Gram Panchayat*	
	Total	*Women*	*Total*	*Women*	*Total*	*Women*
1978	38	2	430	X	2273	X
1983	38	2	427	X	2213	X
1988	38	2	467	4	2586	12
1993	38	13	493	167	2992	1052

From the statement above it can well be perceived that if Govt. of West Bengal had not undertaken such heroic steps for reservation of so far unrepresented segment of the population, women would have never got the scope to come to these people's bodies. In fact this is the boon of the 73rd Amendment to the Constitution, though 1993 election in West Bengal was held before the 73rd Amendment was given effect. The direct effect of this is noticed in women representation as heads of offices in institutions of different tiers e.g. Zilla Parishad at district level, Panchayat Samiti at block level and Gram Panchayat at village level. From the statement on next page this will be clear.

This statement is framed on the basis of the election held in 1993. It clearly reflects the persistent insensitivity towards women. This happened because 1993 election was held before the effect of 73rd Amendment. This would not be the state if election was held after the effect of 73rd Amendment as there is

Women Representation as Heads of Offices in W. Bengal

Sl.No.	*Name of PRI*	*No. of Institutions*	*Women as head of Offices*
1.	Zilla Parishad	16	Nil
2.	Panchayat Samiti	328	8
3.	Gram Panchayat	3222	186

provision for keeping one third seats of office bearers reserved for women in tune with the reservation of seats of different tiers. Whatever be the shortcomings, certainly this is a welcome move for emancipating women from the bondages of their entangled lives.

Objective

The present study has been undertaken with the objective of knowing the social and economic background of women members newly elected to the gram panchayats. This study will also help to form an idea about the emerging women leaders at the grassroots level.

Methodology

With this background the present study has been taken up in Birbhum district of the state of West Bengal. The rationale behind taking up Birbhum District is the composition of the district from the viewpoint of number of administrative units (block). This district is neither a big size district like Midnapore or Burdwan consisting of 54 and 31 blocks respectively nor a small size district like Dakshin Dinajpur with only 7 blocks. Birbhum has 19 blocks comprising of 169-gram panchayats. Again on the basis of administrative hierarchies, these blocks are arranged under three sub-divisions. These sub-divisions are namely Suri Sadar (7 blocks). Bolpur (4 blocks) and Rampurhat (8 blocks). From each sub-division the block with the highest number of gram panchayats was selected for this study. The reason for taking the block with the highest number of gram panchayats is to get more women members for studying. After the selection of the blocks, the women members of all the gram panchayats were taken into consideration for this study.

Distribution of block-wise women members is presented in Table-1. In total 213 women members were taken up for this study (Table-1).

Table-1
Block-wise Distribution of Women Gram Panchayat Members

Sl.No.	*Block*	*No. of Gram Panchayat*	*No. of Women members*	*No. of Women members*	*Percentage of Women members*
1.	Bolpur-Sriniketan	9	193	67	34.71
2.	Sanithia	12	201	70	34.82
3.	Nalhati I	11	212	76	35.85
	Total	32	606	213	35.15

On the basis of a structured questionnaire consisting of relevant information on their socio-economic conditions, women members of all the gram panchayats of the three blocks were interviewed. The information includes their social classification, age, and educational status, land holding pattern, occupational status, per annum income of the family etc.

The Study

Women are classified into four groups on the basis of their social groups viz. Scheduled Castes, Scheduled Tribe, Muslim and other castes. From Table 2 it can be seen that of total 213 members 40.37 percent are from scheduled castes (SC) and 15.49 percent are from scheduled tribe (ST) communities. Both SC and ST together thus covered 55.86 percent of membership. The large number of women members from SC and ST are mainly due to the reservation for SC and ST as the political parties at the time of making nominations tried to nominate in such a manner so that at one stroke both the reservations (for women and SC/ST) be satisfied. Though according to the norms of reservations, one third of the total seats are to be reserved for women, but in the present study 35.15 percent reservations for women are effected. See Table below.

Table-2
Social Group Classification of Women Members

Sl.No.	*Social Groups*	*Bolpur-Sriniketan*	*Sanithia*	*Nalhati I*	*Total*
1.	Scheduled Caste	27	26	33	86
2.	Scheduled Tribe	13	12	8	33
3.	Muslim	12	9	20	41
4.	Other Castes	15	23	14	53
	Total	67	70	76	213

Participation of Muslim women in panchayati raj institutions are very much encouraging as out of 213 total women members of the gram panchayats under the study 41 i.e. 19.24 percent are Muslim. Most of the women members belong to the youngest age group (Table 3).

Table- 3
Age-Social Group Distribution of Women Member

Sl.No.	*Age*	*Scheduled Caste*	*Scheduled Tribe*	*Muslim*	*Other Castes*	*Total*
1.	Upto 30 years	52	21	24	26	123
2.	Above 30 to 45 years	28	11	15	20	74
3	Above 45 to 60 years	6	1	2	5	14
4.	Above 60 years	X	X	X	2	2
	Total	86	33	41	53	213

This signifies that at the time of selection of candidates political parties prefer younger generation to bear the burden of development work in rural areas. 57.75 percent of the total women members under this study belong to the lowest age group. This formation certainly has many good things to contribute, but apprehension is that in male dominated society, as women members are new to the panchayat system, younger women may have every chance to be influenced and dominated by male members who are comparatively experienced and older in generation. A balanced combination of younger and older women members can become good counterparts of male members in the functioning of panchayats. Field level realities also corroborate this apprehension as many women members, during visit to villages, narrated that they were not given sufficient importance during discussions in panchayat meetings (sometimes even their opinions and statements are not noted in resolution). In this study, in the age group up to 45 years there are 92.49 per cent of 213 members while in the case of others it is 87 percent. For SC and Muslim community the corresponding figures are 93 and 95 percent. As the level of education of SC/ST women is comparatively lower than

Table-4

Age and Educational Status Distribution

Sl.No.	*Educational Status*	*Upto 30 yrs*	*Above 30 - 45 yrs*	*Above 45 - 60 yrs*	*Above 60 yrs*	*Total*
1.	Neo literate	18	18	3	X	39
2.	Literate without schooling	12	7	2	1	22
3.	Primary	38	21	8	X	67
4.	Secondary	50	23	X	1	74
5.	Graduate	4	4	X	X	8
6.	Post-Graduate	1	1	1	X	3
	Total	123	74	14	2	213

those belonging to non-SC/ST community, predominance of their number simply results in dominance by male members. It is very much likely that political parties nominate only those of the areas who are not only loyal to them but also possess very low profile. Of 213 members, 39 are neoliterate (Table 4) and of neoliterates SC/ST percentage is 84.61 percent (Table 5).

Table-5
Education Social Group Classification of Members

Sl. No.	*Educational Status*	*Scheduled Caste*	*Scheduled Tribe*	*Muslim Castes*	*Other*	*Total*
1.	Neoliterate	22	11	6	X	39
2.	Literate without schooling	10	9	3	X	22
3.	Primary	32	6	17	12	67
4.	Secondary	21	7	15	31	74
5.	Graduate	1	X	X	7	8
6.	Post-Graduate	X	X	X	3	3
	Total	86	33	41	53	213

Again of neoliterates, 36 i.e.92.30 percent belong to the age group upto 45 years. From the view point of distribution of members on the basis of their ages and educational attainment (Table 4) it can be seen that of the youngest age group 75.61 percent have education up to primary level and above. These women leaders can be a very strong force for betterment of women in rural areas. But field experience tells different stories. These women leaders though have enough potentialities for rendering services but they are not given adequate support either from development bureaucracy or fellow male panchayat members. At the time of discussion with them regarding their feelings about their new panchayat system, most of them complained that they are not getting adequate and proper replies to queries in respect of different development programmes and their implementation process. As a consequence they have to depend blindly on block officials and gram panchayat officials. In the gram panchayat meetings they simply raised their hands up for expressing their consent without questioning. More or less, this is the picture at grass root level after inclusion of sizeable number of women members in the panchayat institutions. In the case of higher qualifications from secondary level and above most of the members (48.23 percent) belong to 'others' group. Of women members from Muslim community 78 percent have education primary and above while in the case of Scheduled Caste members this percentage is 61.62 percent.

Occupational distribution of women members reflects that 46.48 percent members are non-workers (Table 6).

Table 6
Social Group-Occupation Status Distribution.

Sl.No.	*Occupation*	*Scheduled Caste*	*Scheduled Tribe*	*Muslim*	*Other Castes*	*Total*
1.	Cultivator	33	17	X	2	52
2.	Bargadar	5	1	X	2	6
3.	Pattadar	10	8	8	12	38
4.	Animal Husbandry & Agro-industry	3	X	X	X	3
5.	Rural Artisan	X	X	4	1	5
6.	Shop owner	X	X	X	1	1
7.	Other Business	X	X	2	2	4
8.	Teacher	1	X	X	X	1
9.	Other services	1	X	X	X	1
10.	Student	1	X	X	5	6
11.	Housewife	32	7	27	27	93
	Total	86	33	41	53	2

They are mainly engaged in household activities, which are non-paying. The percentage of non-workers is the highest among Muslim community members; the percentage is 65.85 percent (27 out of 41). But in the case of tribal community the percentage is less— it is only 21.22 percent— the lowest among all the social groups. In tribal community both husband and wife work together to earn for their families. Sectoral distribution of activities of women (table 7) shows that of 213 members 46.47 percent members are engaged in primary sector comprising of agriculture and allied activities. Only 5 i.e. 2.35 percent belong to secondary sector and 4.69 percent pursue tertiary sector activities (service business, etc.). In the primary sector representation of SC/ST communities is heavy (77.78 percent) because due to their poor economic conditions they have to depend on agriculture for livelihood. Whereas in tertiary sector representation of non-SC/ST members is eighty percent of which sixty percent members are from SC/ST and non-Muslim community. Less number of members in secondary sector implies that at the time of selecting candidates, people pursuing rural industries are not adequately considered .As a result representation of the people in this sector is very much less in comparison to primary and tertiary sectors. This is true of male members also. Of the total male members of the three study blocks only 4 out of 393 (1.01 percent) depend on the secondary sector for earning.

Table-7
Social Group Activity Sector wise Distribution of Women Members

Sl.N.	*Social Group*	*Primary Sector*	*Secondary Sector*	*Tertiary Sector*	*Non-Working*	*Total*
1.	Schedule Caste	51	X	3	32	86
2.	Schedule Tribes	26	X	X	7	33
3.	Muslim	8	4	2	27	41
4.	Others	14	1	11	27	53
	Total	99	5	16	93	213

Age group distribution of members on the basis of their occupational status (Table 8) reflects that of 99 non-working members out of 213, 91 i.e. 91.91 percent are of age group upto 45 years.

Table-8
Age-Group Occupational Status Distributions.

Sl. No.	*Occupation Status*	*Upto 30 years*	*30 years to 45 years*	*45 years to 60 years*	*Above 60 years*	*Total*
1.	Cultivator	28	20	3	1	52
2.	Bargadar	2	2	2	X	6
3.	Pattadar	21	15	2	X	38
4.	Animal Husbandry & Agro-industry	2	1	X	X	5
5.	Rural Artisan	5	X	X	X	5
6.	Shop owner	1	X	X	X	1
7.	Other Services	X	1	X	X	1
8.	Student	6	X	X	X	6
9.	Housewife	56	29	7	1	93
	Total	123	74	14	2	213

This indicates that potential and productive age groups are confined to the four walls of family when they have to toil hard to manage their families and the new responsibilities entrusted through 73rd Amendment. In the course of field visit to the villages many women members complained that they were not getting full support form their family members including their husbands because no redistribution of family works resulted due to this epoch making decision to bring women into the mainstream of decision making and implementation process of development activities.

Information on land holding of the families of women members was collected with the purpose of knowing from which class these women leaders are coming. Above forty five percent of women members themselves depend on land for earning. Of total 213 members, 89 i.e.41.78 percent is landless, which means that these families have no land of their own. 38 members of the total 213 members (17.84 percent) are classified as *pattadar* as they received ceiling surplus land from the state government. But not in a single case these *pattas* are recorded jointly with husband and wife or in the name of female members of the families (very recently Government of West Bengal has taken the decision to distribute *pattas* in the name of husband and wife). In this study (Table 9) it is shown that *pattadars* received land from the Government, and in other cases of category of land holding land is of their own either they acquire it or it is inherited.

Table-9

Political Party Landholding Distribution of members.

Sl. No.	*Landholding Status*	*BJP*	*Cong (I)*	*CPI*	*CPI (M)*	*Others*	*Total*
1.	Landless	8	9	2	65	5	89
2.	Pattadar	X	1	1	35	1	38
3.	Upto 2.5	2	12	1	37	8	60
4.	Above 2.5 to 5.0	1	3	1	16	1	22
5.	Above 5.0 to 10.0	2	X	X	1	1	4
6.	Above 10.0	X	X	X	X	X	X
	Total	13	25	5	154	16	213

Land-holding status distribution of women members shows that 28.17 percent members belong to marginal farmers category, while 10.33 percent are small farmers. This distribution indicates that in the lowest strata of panchayat raj set up in West Bengal representation of landed gentry is very thin only 12.20 percent of the total women gram panchayat members in three blocks (under study) have holding size in the range of small farmers and above. Political party-wise distribution of members on the basis of landholding pattern (as framed in Table 9) reflects that all the political parties tried to nominate poor families with little landed property for running the gram panchayats. Certainly here lies the uniqueness of West Bengal Panchayat System where political parties are making efforts to make these bodies truly representative and to free them from the clutches of wealthier people so that these bodies can work effectively for the poor. In BJP there are the highest number of landless women members (Table 9 a) followed by CPI (M). From this point of view, there are no major differences in the approaches of different political parties. See Table (9 a) below.

Table-9 (a)

Representation of members in political parties (In percentage) the basis of landholding

Sl. No.	*Political Party*	*Landless*	*Pattadar 2.5*	*Upto 2.5 to 5.0*	*Above 5.0 to 10.0*	*Above*	*Total*
1.	CPI(M)	42.20	9.74	37.01	10.40	0.65	100.00
2.	CPI	40.00	20.00	20.00	20.00	X	100.00
3.	Cong (I)	36.00	4.00	48.00	12.00	X	100.00
4.	BJP	61.54	X	15.38	7.70	15.38	100.00
5.	Others	31.25	6.25	50.00	6.25	6.25	100.00
	Total	210.99	39.99	170.39	56.35	22.28	500.00

Lastly distribution of members on the basis of their political affiliation and educational attainment is shown in table 10.

From the table it can be seen that 23.37 percent of CPI (M) members are simply neoliterate while only 12 percent of Congress (1) members are neoliterate (Table-10a).

Table-10
Political Party and Education Status.

Sl.No.	*Education Status*	*BJP*	*Cong (I)*	*CPI*	*CPI (M)*	*Others*	*Total*
1.	Illiterate	X	X	X	X	X	X
2.	Neo Literate	X	3	X	36	X	39
3.	Literate without Schooling	2	X	3	13	4	22
4.	Primary	7	11	2	40	7	67
5.	Secondary	4	8	X	58	4	74
6.	Graduate	X	2	X	5	1	8
7.	Post Graduate	X	1	X	2	X	3
	Total	13	25	5	154	16	213

This may indicate that CPI (M) nominated such candidates who have very low educational profile due to which they may remain subdued in the course of discharging their functions. If the last three rungs of educational attainments be added together, then it can be seen that of total 154 CPI (M) members 57.79 percent belong to this group while 56 percent of Congress (I) members belong to this group. In the case of BJP this figure is a bit higher (69.23 percent). Again if the three higher educational qualifications be taken into account, there also differences-between congress (I) and CPI (M) are very much insignificant. Of CPI (M) members 42.22 percent belong to qualification range from secondary to postgraduate while the corresponding figure in case of Congress (I) is 44 percent. To make women members really strong it is expected that political parties should nominate such women who have the capability to reach the level where they can influence the decision-making and implementation proves at gram panchayat level.

Some educational qualification is a must for acquiring this capability. Otherwise whatever is the pious intention, women will not be benefited to a great extent and the prevailing situation will continue. This merely contradicts the intentions of the 73rd Amendment Act.

Table-10 (a)

Representation of Different Education class in political parties

Sl.No	Political Party	Neo-literate	Literate	Primary	Secon-dary	Graduate	Post Graduate	Total
1.	BJP	X	15.38	53.85	30.77	X	X	100.00
2.	Cong (I)	12.00	X	44.00	32.00	8.00	4.00	100.00
3.	CPI	X	69.00	40.00	X	X	X	100.00
4.	CPI (M)	23.37	8.44	25.97	37.66	3.26	1.30	100.00
5.	Others	X	25.00	43.75	25.00	6.25	X	100.00
	Total	35.37	117.82	207.57	125.43	17.51	5.30	500.00

CONCLUSION

On the force of the 73rd Amendment Act women were brought to the Panchayat Raj Institutions. Hence they are very new to the system. They require lot of back-up support not only from the rural development administration, particularly block level bureaucracy, but also from the experienced and senior members. Government of West Bengal has taken up a scheme for providing training to all members of the three tier institutions. For women office bearers separate training programmes were organised. But one-time training will not prove sufficient for women members, as most of them are totally new to the system. Organizing training at block level at least once a year will be helpful to women members for strengthening their knowledge base. In addition to official training, political parties should take up a plan for training of these emerging young leaders on continuous basis so that they can learn from experiences of working. So far progress in this respect is not satisfactory as many women members told during interview that even after two years of coming to the panchayat bodies most of the things remain new to them and they have to depend on officials of gram panchayats and blocks for each and every activity. This situation needs to be changed at any cost. Otherwise the basic philosophy behind bringing women to the panchayat bodies will be frustrated. At the block level, block administration, in particular block development officer and officer-in-charge of panchayat affairs, have great role to play in making the women members self-sufficient by acting as source of knowledge and inspiration for them. Until and unless these new leaders are empowered adequately, empowerment of rural women will remain a distant dream.

SUGGESTED REFERENCES

Lieten, G.K., 'Panchayat Leaders in West Bengal, EPW, Oct. 1, 1988.

Saxena, K.B., 'Pamchayats and Women', Kurukshetra, 1989.

Index

A

Administrative infrastructure, 69

APO as a,
  awareness builder, 72
  coordinator, 71
  facilitator, 71
  motivator, 71
  planner and manager, 71
  source of information, 71

Assam Tribune, 9

Asset formation,
  and income generation, 91

Asset utilization pattern,
  impact of literacy on, 90

B

Batra, S.L., 30

Beneficiaries,
  awareness of, 87
  literacy status, 82

C

Census of India, 11, 18

Committee on Status of Women,
  Report of, 54

Constitution 73rd Amendment
  Act, 109

Constitution 73rd Amendment
  Act, 1992, 5

72nd and 73rd Constitutional
  amendments, 2, 30

D

District Census Handbook, 10

DRDA, 65, 67, 68

Dreze, Jean, 32

Dutta, S.K., 81

DWCRA, 3, 4, 53, 54-63, 66-67
  coverage of programme, 50

E

Economic activities, 66

Eighth Five Year Plan, 30

F

Female workforce,
  age structure of, 25
  sectoral breakup of, 20, 21

Female-headed households
  (FHH),
  assets of, 43
  caste breakup of, 38
  household formation, 35
  income of, 47
  literacy status, 39
  objectives, 33
  occupational status and
    earning members, 40
  operational existence of, 34

sex ratio of, 36
status, 2, 32-

G

Ghosh, D.K., 81
Gram sevika, 70
Groups and members,
growth of, 56

H

Human Development Report, 8

I

ICDS, 76
Income aspect, 42
Income generation impact, 92
Indian Factories Act, 18
Investment, quantum of,
and pre-assistance income,
85
IRDP, 2, 53, 67, 86
access of beneficiaries to skill
development, 93

J

JRY, 54, 69

L

Lauback, Frank, 79
Literacy scenario, 81

P

Prasad, C.H., 53
Production aspect, 42

R

Reddy, S., 53
Reorganisation aspect, 42
Revolving fund, 62
Rural femal workforce,
breakup of, 18
Rural women,
work participation rates of, 10

S

Self employment scheme,
option for, 48
Swaminathan, M.S., 8

T

Total Literacy Campaign, 95
Training,
an essential input, 72
TRYSEM, 55, 67, 93

U

UNICEF, 55

W

Women,
empowerment of through
literacy, 4
in Panchayat, 5
policies and programmes
related to, 3, 53-78
Women empowerment through
literacy, 79-85
Women in Panchayat, 96-110
Women workers,
classification, 16
Women workforce,
objectives of study, 9
profile of, 2, 8-31
Workers classifications,
by education level, 22
WPR, 13

❑❑❑